GRIGOR'S OBSESSION

Matt Oberon's screenplay©
based on
the novella "Delusion"
by ©Derek Thomas

Published by Mercutio Books
Simon's Town
South Africa
27 21 7861356

ISBN: 978-1492324768

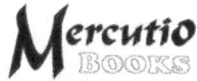

MAIN CHARACTERS

Grigor Sidorov	Art historian with the Russian State art treasury
Mariya Ivanovskaya Sidorova	Grigor's grandmother, mentor and inspiration
Anatoly Danilovich Sidorov	Grigor's grandfather, and the link with his ancestry
Mikhail Ivanovich	Grigor's lifelong friend
Ada	Grigor's wife
Vovo	Street boy and pickpocket, and Grigor's accomplice
Lara	Grigor's lover and accessory
Stroganov	Curator of the Peterhof Palace St Petersburg
Skuratov	Security Head of SRP for State art treasures

GRIGOR'S OBSESSION

The story takes place in Russia in the post-Soviet era
with references to the past, back to Peter the Great.

EXT. TAXI RANK AT ST PETERSBURG PULKOVO AIRPORT - DAY

An altercation takes place between the taxi driver and
Grigor Sidorov, the passenger, after he has alighted.

>   GRIGOR
>   (indignant)
>   You can't be serious. You said
>   it would be one hundred roubles
>   all the way. Now you want more.
>   Forget it.

>   TAXI DRIVER
>   I had to take the long route as
>   the traffic blocked with roads.

>   GRIGOR
>   That may be, but that's your
>   problem. Here's your money. Take
>   it or leave it!

>   TAXI DRIVER
>   We'll meet again, mister.

INT. THE AIRPORT TERMINAL - DAY

Grigor leaves taxi and enters the terminal. After
perestroika the airports have become overcrowded with
Russians travelling at will for the first time, some of
them on business, like Grigor, and returning to Moscow.
But worse than the jostling of the crowds is stream of
flight announcements which assault the ears.

Grigor finds a seat, sits and waits. There is little else
to do but ponder about the lives of his fellow
travellers, each living in a private coccoon and
remaining strangers to one another. His flight is
announced and he rushes forward to join the quickforming
queue. It moves forward very slowly. He hears a woman's
voice speaking loudly to airport security.

>   WOMAN
>   I told you it is not mine! There
>   was a man sitting here a while
>   go. Do you think this is a bomb?

                    SECURITY OFFICER
          We can never be sure...

Grigor turns and sees that his red canister, which he
forgot about, is the object of the discussion. He leaves
the queue and chases after the security officer.

                    GRIGOR
               (he tugs at the
                canister)
          Officer, officer...this is
          mine...I left it behind when
          I...

                    SECURITY OFFICER
               (turns and studies
                Grigor)
          You seem very concerned, sir. Is
          there anything you want to tell
          me?

                    GRIGOR
          Look, it's simple. I rushed to
          join the queue and forgot to
          pick this up with my other bags.

                    SECURITY OFFICER
               (opens the canister)
          Can you tell me what's inside?

                    GRIGOR
          Just paintings.

                    SECURITY OFFICER
          Paintings? Your paintings? Do
          you have work?

                    GRIGOR
          Yes, I work for the State in the
          art restoration department.

                    SECURITY OFFICER
          So these paintings are State
          treasures?

                    GRIGOR
          No! No! These are my own
          paintings.

A crowd has gathered. The Security officer removes the
canvases and unrolls them, then shows them to the crowd.

                    CROWD
               (appreciative)
          Oooh...

                    SECURITY OFFICER
          You are a good painter, sir.
          But, I think that you must let
          me have your details. Come this
          way.

The security officer leads still holding the canister and
Grigor follows.

INT. THE AIRPORT TERMINAL - DAY

Grigor is back in the queue, his canister returned to
him.

                    GRIGOR (O.C.)
               (checks the red
                canister)
          You're a fool, Grigor, to leave
          your paintings unattended.
          Things could have gone horribly
          wrong. Best not to think about
          the next move. The risk will be
          great, but I owe it to Masha, to
          restore the family to its
          rightful place in the history of
          this great country. A pity it
          has to be this way.

The queue moves on. Grigor hands his ticket to the
airline ticket clerk, a country girl with too much make-
up. She flashes her heavy black lashes at him.

                    TICKET CLERK
          You travel by air a lot, mister
          Grigor... Sidorov. How do you
          spend your time in St
          Petersburg? Alone?

                    GRIGOR
          Sometimes...

                    TICKET CLERK
          (hands back his ticket)
          Well, I can change all that.

                    GRIGOR
          I have girlfriend.

                    TICKET CLERK
          Lucky girl. That's a pity. Go
          through to the departure lounge.
          Next.

She watches him depart, dressed not like any other State
employee, more like a man with culture, who walks with
dignity.

                                        CUT TO:

INT. THE AIRPORT DEPARTURE LOUNGE - DAY

Grigor takes a seat in the crowded waiting lounge, the
flight announcements continue unabated. In defence he
gets lost in his thoughts.

                    GRIGOR (O.C.)
          On my next visit Petersburg I
          will go and find that young
          pickpocket Vovo, who nearly
          stole my paintings on the Metro.
          I know he'll still be lifting
          the pockets of the passengers at
          Nevsky Prospekt. Young
          opportunist. But that street
          wisdom of his is going to be
          useful for the next part of the
          plan.

The flight is announced. The waiting passengers all stand
and move to the boarding exit.

                    GRIGOR (O.C.)
                 (joins the queue)
          Am I insane to go through with
          this mission which has every
          chance of failure?

TWENTY YEARS EARLIER

INT. RAILWAY CARRIAGE - DAY

Drawn by a steam train on its way between Moscow and
Kolomenskoye, Alexandr Sidorov and his wife Natalya and
their children, Grigor and his sister Luisa, travel in a
carriage to spend the weekend at their grandmother's
dacha. It is springtime and the children are getting
excited and play a noisy game of 'I spy'.

                    NATALYA
          Shush, now. People will think
          you're not taught how to behave!

They continue as though they haven't heard.

                    ALEXANDR
               (looks over the
               newspaper)
          Did you hear what your mother
          said, Grigor? And Luisa, you're
          older and should be setting an
          example.

                    LUISA & GRIGOR
          Yes, Pappa.

                    GRIGOR
          Will Masha be at the station,
          Pappa?

                    ALEXANDR
          No, Grigor. It is too far to the
          station for your babushka to
          meet you. Be patient, you'll see
          her very soon.

They settle quietly into watching the passing landscape.
The train pulls into the station. There is much steam,
and passengers bustle along the platform.

                                        CUT TO:

EXT. THE KOLOMENSKOYE STATION FORECOURT - DAY

The Sidorovs find an open horsecart driven by a young man
who helps load their bags.

                    ALEXANDR
               (to the driver)
          Oho, Pyotr, here we are again.
          Good weather at last! *Spesibo*.

                    PYOTR
          My pleasure. Yes, the weather is
          its own master. Will it be to
          Mariya Sidorova's dasha as
          usual?

                    ALEXANDR
          As usual. *Spesibo*.

                                        FADE TO:

EXT. AT MARIYA SIDOROVA'S DACHA - DAY
The dacha is set in a clearing in a birch forest with
other dachas. It is of the typical vernacular kind,
wooden structure, with painted fretted surrounds to the

windows. Neat rows of newly planted vegetables adjoin
each house, and thin curls of smoke from the chimneys.

Mariya is standing at the doorway of her dacha. She waves
with a handkerchief. The children leap off the horsecart
and run to her open arms. There is much hugging while
Alexandr and Pyotr unload the bags.

>   MARIYA
>   Aah...your Masha has been
>   waiting to spoil you again. But
>   first some refreshment, then I
>   have a surprise for you.

The family all greet then enter the house.

EXT. IN MARIYA'S VEGETABLE PATCH - DAY

Grigor and his friend, Mikhail Ivanovich (Misha), are
helping his babushka to dig over the soil.

>   GRIGOR
>   Masha. Tell me about grandfather
>   Anatoly. Why was he killed?

>   MARIYA
>   Oh, Grigor. You are so young to
>   want to know about such things.

>   GRIGOR
>   Was he killed because he didn't
>   want to be in the Revolution?

>   MARIYA
>   That was part of it. Look I've
>   found the last of the potatoes.

>   GRIGOR
>   What was grandfather like?

>   MARIYA
>   He was a noble person, a gentle
>   man. He believed that he was a
>   descendant from one of the most
>   noble families of Russia. But
>   that's a story for when you are
>   a bit older, Grigor.

>   CUT TO:

EXT. MARIYA SIDOROVA'S DACHA - DAY

Grigor and his friend Misha, short for Mikhail, are
building mock-ups of kremlins, mounting parades with toy
soldiers and imagining they are Russian princes at war
with one another.

                    ALEXANDR
          (from the doorway)
          You must come inside now Grigor
          and get Misha to help you bring
          wood for the stove.

                                        FADE OUT.

INT. MARIYA SIDOROVA'S DACHA - NIGHT

The family are seated around the table and eating. The
enormous tiled stove in the corner warms the space.

                    GRIGOR
          Masha says that grandfather was
          noble man. Does that mean he was
          from a noble family?

His parents and Mariya exchange looks.

                    ALEXANDR
          He believed he was, Grigor. Now
          eat your *pirozhki* that Masha has
          made for us.

Grigor takes a mouthful.

                    GRIGOR
          But, why did they kill noble
          men?

                    LUISA
          You're so inquisitive! And too
          young to be allowed to know
          everything.

                    GRIGOR
          (looks sternly at his
            sister)
          I'm old enough to know. Don't
          treat me like a baby.

Mariya rises from the table, collects the empty plates.
They all rise and make themselves comfortable close to
the stove. Grigor and Misha, his friend, lie down on the
floor and eavesdrop on the conversation of the adults.

                    ALEXANDR
          What have you done with the seal
          Masha?

                    MARIYA
          It's in safe keeping. Maryna
          still hasn't got over finding my
          Anatoly in the morgue. Poor
          girl.

                    NATALYA
          A miracle she found the seal
          still in his clenched fist.

                                        INSERT:

INT. STATE MORTUARY - NIGHT

Maryna, Mariya Sidorova's daughter, is being shown into a
room in the mortuary where she sees the body of her
father, Anatoly. She kneels and weeps over his body, then
takes his clenched hand in hers and it holds a something
unexpectd: an amber seal. She removes it, looks briefly
at it and conceals it, then stands and acknowledges that
it is the body of her father, Anatoly Danilovich Sidorov.

                                        BACK TO:

INT. MARIYA SIDOROVA'S DACHA - NIGHT

                    MARIYA
          It was indeed a miracle. They
          had stripped him of everything,
          even of his rank, but had
          overlooked the one thing he had
          left, the proof of his noble
          origins, the amber seal.

Grigor sits up.

                    GRIGOR
          Aunt Maryna says he was a White
          Russian and wouldn't do what the
          Bolsheviks told him to do.

                    ALEXANDR
          They wanted everyone to join the
          Revolution, otherwise they took
          all their property away.

                    GRIGOR
          Did they shoot grandfather
          Anatoly?

                    NATALYA
          Grigor!

                    ALEXANDR
          No. Now we must tell him. He was
          shot by firing squad, Grigor. He
          was labelled a White Russian
          because he would not cooperate
          with the Revolutionists, do what
          they say, like kill people.
          Because grandfather was a
          pacifist, he abhorred violence
          and was a proud man. His name
          tag was stripped from his tunic
          as if he wasn't worthy, and
          should die nameless. But he had
          the last word, he kept his name
          and the Menshikov amber seal,
          his link with his past.

                    NATALYA
          Those were wicked times.

                    GRIGOR
          Why was the amber seal important
          to granddad, Pappa?

                    ALEXANDR
          Well, he believed that he had
          become the custodian of proof
          that the Sidorovs are
          descendents of the noble
          Menshikovs. He did not share his
          secret except with a few of us
          inside his close family. The
          Bolsheviks decided that he
          wouldn't ever join their cause.

                    GRIGOR
          Who was Menshikov?

                    NATALYA
          Grigor you ask too many
          questions.

                    ALEXANDR
          No. Let me explain. Prince
          Alexandr Danilovich Menshikov
          was close to the seat of power
          at the time of Peter the Great,
          in fact he was Peter's one time
          favourite.

                    MARIYA
          After the Bolshevik revolution
                    (MORE)

                    MARIYA (CONT'D)
        of 1917, my Anatoly was stripped
        of all his possessions, and we
        were left destitute. My little
        dacha became our home. You can
        be proud, Grigor, of your
        grandfather's courage, and the
        legacy of your family line.

                    GRIGOR
        I am, Masha, I am.

                                        FADE OUT.

BACK TO THE PRESENT
Grigor and Misha are twenty years older. Due to his
natural gift for art, Grigor enrolls first at the Lyceum
and then at the Moscow State Academy Art Institute. Misha
embarks on a career in engineering at another institute.
They meet regularly and their childhood friendship is
strong, sustained through their mutual affection for each
other.

                                        JUMPCUT:

INT. A STUDENT COFFEE BAR - DAY
It is the first academic semester for Grigor at the
Academy He bubbles over to Misha about the new art
faculty where he would be spending some years and where
prominent artists from the People's Artists of Russia and
Members of the Russian Academy of Arts were in every day
contact and mentored the students.

                    GRIGOR
        Misha, don't look now, but that
        girl over there modelled for us
        this morning, with no clothes on
        and in this cold weather. I felt
        like putting my arms...I mean
        coat ...around her.

                    MISHA
        Whoa, my friend, I know what's
        on your mind. You're letting you
        imagination run ahead of you...

                    GRIGOR
        Only to be considerate, Misha!

                    MISHA
        Anyway, who is she? She looks
        quite a few years older than
        you.

                    GRIGOR
          Maybe there was nothing in it,
          but I thought she kept smiling
          at me during the poses.

                    MISHA
          Your wishing and hoping is going
          to be your undoing, my friend.
          Do you know her name?

                    GRIGOR
          I think it is Ada.

EXT. SOUVENIR STAND NEAR RED SQUARE - DAY
It is winter and the ground is thick with snow. Misha
sees Ada behind the stall selling tourist souvenirs,
mementoes of Russia, matriochkas, and snow scenes in
glass eggs with St Basil's cathedral in miniature inside.

Misha stands aside for a while watching Ada selling to
customers.

                    MISHA (V.O.)
          Grigor chooses well. She is
          indeed a looker, with a fine
          body to match. No wonder he's
          smitten, and knows much more
          about her now than just her
          name.

Grigor arrives unexpectedly.

                    GRIGOR
          Misha. What are you doing here?

                    MISHA
          I was passing and saw Ada, so
          thought I might buy a souvenir.

                    GRIGOR
          Hands off, my friend.

                    MISHA
          You've fallen for her, haven't
          you?

                    GRIGOR
          We're in love! Maybe I can take
          her away from this boring job
          one day. She has little
          schooling and has been helping
          her family working since she was
                    (MORE)

                    GRIGOR (CONT'D)
          fifteen. At least the modelling
          job at the Academy gives her a
          little extra for small luxuries
          for herself. Come and meet her.

They go to the stall. Grigor kisses her passionately and
Misha meets Ada.

                    GRIGOR (CONT'D)
          Let's go and have coffee Misha
          before I go to the Academy.

They walk across Red Square to a restaurant near the
Eagle Gate.

                                        CUT TO:

INT. A RESTAURANT - DAY

They find a seat at the bar.

                    MISHA
          How is your grandmother, Mariya
          Sidorova?

                    GRIGOR
          We still write to each other
          every week. My beloved babushka
          is my mentor, Misha, and
          encourages my art. There are
          only a few Sidorovs who have
          gone on to higher learning. But
          there is one amongst the alumni
          at the Academy, a noted artist
          with a world reputation.

                    MISHA
          I'm sure you'll live up to the
          family's expectations, my
          friend.

                    GRIGOR
          Today is one of my favourite
          days. We spend the whole day at
          the 'Tretya' studying the work
          of the masters, you know, Andrei
          Rublev's icons, Ilya Repin's and
          Malyavin's enormous paintings...

                    MISHA
          You're losing me, my friend. I
                    (MORE)

                    MISHA (CONT'D)
only know about the famous
"Virgin of Vladimir", which was
moved from the Kremlin to the
Tretyakov some years ago. Now
there is only a copy in the
Kremlin. It was in the papers.

                    GRIGOR
Yes, but the important thing,
Misha, is that it depicts the
Virgin and Child with
exceptional reverence and
humanity where earlier icons
were symbolised by austerity and
severity. I can feel the
painter's passion by just
looking at it. Here, look this
is my copy from the original of
the Virgin.

Grigor opens a folder to show Misha his own depiction of
the Virgin which he had completed on his last visit to
the gallery. His painting, copied from the original, is
an exceptional representation of the beloved of all
icons, venerated for centuries as the guardian and
protector of Holy Russia.

                    MISHA
You have chosen the right
profession, Grigor.

                    GRIGOR
And what's more, I found a
painting in the Tretyakov
gallery by Vasily Surikov of
Prince Alexandr Menshikov and
his daughters in exile in
Beryotov, Siberia. He is
surrounded by his young family,
and depicts the man fallen from
grace, and forced into living in
humble circumstances. To me it
was like finding another piece
in the puzzle, which makes me
determined to uncover my
family's ancestry.

                    MISHA
Did I tell you I did some
research in the State archives?

                    GRIGOR
Come on, tell. About what?

MISHA
About your ancestor, Prince
Alexandr Danilovich Menshikov.
He was an opportunist, only a
vendor of *pirozhki* and a pastry-
cook's assistant.

GRIGOR
So? That changes nothing.

MISHA
Aah, but his was a success
story. It seems likely that his
fortune and his future lay more
in his good looks and a kind of
street smartness which gained
him the attention of the Russian
court. He proved himself as a
resourceful young man and after
his successful cavalry raids
under Peter's command, he was
elevated to the ranks of Prince
and Field-Marshal.

GRIGOR
You rouse my curiosity.

MISHA
But, for your information.
although Peter the Great
preferred women to men, he
shared an intimate relationship
with your ancestor.

GRIGOR
So what, Misha!

MISHA
He rose as if to the manner born
to his privileged life but
eventually fell from grace. For
his wilfulness he earned the
wrath of the Tzar. The more I
read, the more one becomes won
over by the indomitable
Menshikov. He was an elegant
rogue who succumbed to the human
failing of lapses of good sense
and occasionally stepped over
the boundaries of honesty.

GRIGOR
I want to hear more, Misha. But
now I must go.

Grigor packs his things.

                    GRIGOR (CONT'D)
          Goodbye my friend.

                    MISHA
          I'll see you soon, 'Grigor the
          Great'!

Grigor hugs his friend and leaves. Misha stays.

                    MISHA (V.O.)
          I came away from my readings
          almost forgiving the man
          Menshikov, who, having risen
          from modest origins and become
          the favourite of Peter the
          Great, made a Prince and a
          governor-general with almost
          unlimited powers, must have been
          highly persuasive and skilful to
          have had his name perpetuated in
          the complex web of Russian
          history. If Menshikov's genes
          indeed run strongly in the veins
          of the Sidorovs, what possible
          chance of restitution can there
          be for the Sidorovs?

                                        DISSOLVE:

INT. STAIRCASE IN GRIGOR'S MOSCOW STUDIO ROOM - DAY
The staircase is in a pre-Soviet building with apartments
overlooking a courtyard.

Grigor climbs with parcels to the top floor, dressed
heavily for winter. He is out of breath when he reaches
the door of his attic studio.

                                        CUT TO:

INT. GRIGOR'S ATTIC STUDIO - DAY

Grigor offloads the parcels on to the heavily scrubbed
table, then busies himself tidying up the space expecting
Ada to arrive. He hears a noise from the stairs, and she
opens the door.

                    ADA
          Grigor! Hello my love. These
          stairs seem worse every time.
          But at least with the bursary
                    (MORE)

                         ADA (CONT'D)
          from the Academy you have a
          place where you can paint
          uninterrupted.

                         GRIGOR
          But I like interruptions...only
          if you are causing them.

He rushes to help her with her coat which is sprinkled
with snow flakes, and kisses her passionately.

                         GRIGOR (CONT'D)
          Come sit. I've got some good red
          wine, and I thought I'd better
          get something eat with it. Your
          favourite...*pirozhki* with a meat
          filling.

                         ADA
          Why are you so good to me,
          Grigor?

                         GRIGOR
          Because you're like a kitten.
          You purr and live in the moment.

                         ADA
          Do you love me?

Grigor pauses before answering.

                         GRIGOR
          I believe so.

                         ADA
              (petulantly)
          That's not good enough! What is
          the problem?

                         GRIGOR
              (hesitating)
          I haven't told anyone yet, but I
          am having strange sensations.
          Everytime I go to the Tretyakov
          gallery and study the masters,
          something tells me that there
          are more important for me to be
          doing. I have been
          introspective, Ada, my pretty
          love. I'm sorry.

                         ADA
              (hugs and kisses him)
          I think I can forgive you.

                    GRIGOR
          I also have this desire to paint
          you. Can you sit still for just
          a half an hour for me to capture
          the essence of your beauty, the
          smoothness and even tone of your
          skin? Here under the window.

Grigor has already prepared a place on the divan under
the dormer window through which St Basil on Red Square
can be seen in the far distance.

                    ADA
          It's too cold Grigor!

                    GRIGOR
          Let me build up the stove.

He stokes the stove and places more logs in it.

                    GRIGOR (CONT'D)
                    (goes to the divan)
          Come, I would like you to pose
          here. But Ada, my love, your
          clothes hide too much of you.
          I'll arrange this drape so that
          you are not so cold with them
          off.

Grigor moves his canvas into position. He studies his
subject, Ada, then arranges the drape and brings her
flowing hair over her shoulder. He takes a scarf and
gathers it tightly around her head to show off her
features.

                    ADA
          How long is this going to take,
          Grigor?

                    GRIGOR
          Not long.

Grigor picks up his brushes and palette and starts to
paint.

                                        FADE OUT.

                                        FADE TO:

                    ADA
          I keep hoping, Grigor, that you
          will take me to the country to
          meet your *babushka*. You have
          told me so much about her and
                    (MORE)

                    ADA (CONT'D)
          her little dacha. You write to
          her every week, and I want to
          meet the woman who can command
          your affection. I have met your
          parents, but I really do want to
          meet your grandmother.

                    GRIGOR
               (absorbed with his
                painting)
          You will, you will...

                                        DISSOLVE:

                                        BACK TO:

INT. GRIGOR'S ATTIC STUDIO - NIGHT
Grigor has completed the painting.

Ada rises, wraps herself in a blanket and goes across to
view the painting.

                    ADA
          Grigor, that's the best you have
          ever done of me. It is
          beautiful... I seem to be
          floating in another world. How
          clever you are!

                    GRIGOR
               (hugs Ada)
          That means more to me than
          compliments at the Academy.
          Come, now we must eat.

They light candles and heat up the *pirozhki* on the stove.
They warm the red wine, and sit down. Their eyes are
fixated on each other. First Grigor, then Ada smiles
before they clutch each other and kiss passionately.
Grigor leads Ada to the divan, where they strip and make
love.

                                        DISSOLVE:

                                        BACK TO:

INT. GRIGOR'S ATTIC STUDIO - NIGHT

There is a loud knock on the door.

                         GRIGOR
                  Stay quiet...

Another loud knock. Grigor gets up pulls on a coat and
goes to the door.

                         GRIGOR (CONT'D)
                  Who's there?

                         MISHA
                  Grigor, it's me, Misha. Open up
                  I have something to tell you.

Grigor unlatches the door and Misha rushes in. He sees
immediately that he is intruding, but has important news.

                         MISHA (CONT'D)
                       (takes Grigor by the
                        shoulders)
                  I have bad news, my dear friend.
                  Your babushka...

                         GRIGOR
                       (instantly)
                  No, no, no!

                         MISHA
                  Yes, Grigor. She died this
                  morning and they contacted me
                  from her dacha because you don't
                  have a telephone.

Grigor falls on Misha and hugs him, then pushes him away
and goes to sit at the table. Ada consoles him as he sobs
uncontrollably.

                                             FADE OUT.

                                             FADE TO:

INT. MARIYA SIDOROVA'S DACHA - DAY
In the small room at the front, Mariya's plain birchwood
coffin is open so that all who came to pay their respects
and view the body and take their leave. Her arms hold
fading flowers from her garden and are crossed over her
chest.

Around the coffin mourners lay their offerings, amongst
them, coloured Easter eggs, the expression of a rite
called Khristósovanie. It is the late afternoon, just
as the sun is showing its last rays through the
windows.

                              MISHA (V.O.)
                    Mariya Sidorova has lined her
                    coffin with the fabrics which
                    she herself embroidered during
                    her later years. The fading
                    flowers are from her garden and
                    crossed over her chest as though
                    she claimed the fertility of the
                    soil from which they had grown
                    and from which she had drawn
                    sustenance throughout her
                    hardworking life. She alone must
                    have brought the coffin down
                    from the attic, no mean feat for
                    one nearing death. Then she
                    carefully arranged the cottage
                    so that the first person to find
                    her would not feel compelled to
                    tidy up.

The priest calls Grigor to one side. In his hand is small
handmade box inside of which was an embroidered linen
wrapping with Mariya's immaculate stitching of 'Grigor
Anatoly Sidorov' in one corner.

                              PRIEST
                    A blessing on you Grigor Sidorov
                    during this time of grief.

Grigor sobs.

                              GRIGOR
                    Why didn't she call me?

                              PRIEST
                    She didn't want you to know of
                    her terminal illness. She
                    believed it would detract from
                    the quality of your discourse in
                    your weekly letters. Your
                    babushka asked me to keep this
                    box and give it only to you.

With the tears flowing, Grigor opens it, and draws out a
letter. In her own laboured handwriting Mariya Sidorova
had written her simple last will and testament:

                              MARIYA (O.S.)
                    "To Grigor Anatoly Sidorov, my
                    grandson. You must forgive your
                    loving babushka, and pray for
                    her. She did not want to burden
                    you with the ailments of the
                    past year which entered her
                              (MORE)

                    MARIYA (O.S.)
body. Your letters to me every
week were my lifeblood, and your
young life an inspiration to
this old soul. Of all the
Sidorovs, you are the one who
can carry the name forward and
uphold and restore its dignity
after the sacrifices of your
noble forebears. The family has
it roots in history and as you
know, your grandfather, Anatoly,
when he died so tragically, held
in his hand a symbol of the
pride he felt about his
ancestry, the amber seal of the
Menshikovs. With this box, your
grandmother passes the seal to
you, my Grigor, for safekeeping
and for whatever inspiration you
draw from it. My dacha has been
my haven, my little kremlin,
against the changes of the
outside world. It has sheltered
me through the seasons, and my
small garden has provided me
with food on the table. I leave
them behind with great sadness.
But it would hurt less if I was
to know that you, Grigor, were
the owner and would look after
my dear cottage and work the
garden, as I did, as we did
together from when you were a
little boy. The dacha and all
its contents are yours and I
give them with my all my heart,
because I can trust you. In your
favour, your father Alexandr,
and your aunt, Maryna, have
declined to have the property. I
have a little money, not much,
but it will also help you to
keep the little home in good
repair, but the rest you will
need to add. Your grandmother is
sure that you will be recognised
as a great artist one day and
money will not be a problem.
Through this letter, you are the
last person I have spoken to,
and that has been my wish.
God take care of you, my Grigor
the Great. Mariya Ivanovskaya
Sidorova."

Ada puts her hand on grief-stricken Grigor, his shoulders
shake with emotion.

                    MISHA (V.O.)
          He is unable to express into
          words how he feels at this
          moment, or to fully comprehend
          the extent of his loss of his
          beloved babushka. But I can and
          I view the outpouring of grief
          from my friend with foreboding
          that without his soul's anchor,
          his otherwise whimsical
          temperament could be transformed
          by the tragedy. Mariya
          Sidorova's roots belong to the
          country, the town Rostov Veliky
          on lake Nero, where she grew up.
          It is some hours on the
          elektrichka train from Moscow.
          That was where she has chosen to
          be buried. When the Soviet
          government confiscated the
          properties of Anatoly and
          rendered the family almost
          destitute, she willingly came
          with her husband to the dacha at
          Kolomenskoye, but her heart was
          still in Rostov where the
          remains of her forebears lie.
          Her body will be sent by train
          tomorrow and the family would
          accompany it. Mariya Sidorova
          was a woman of great compassion
          and beauty even in her latter
          years because of it. The hot
          soups...*borsch* was my
          favourite...and *pirozhki* breads
          she made for us when were
          growing up symbolised the warmth
          and kindness of her very being.

                                        FADE OUT.

                                        FADE TO:

INT. ON BOARD THE TRAIN TO ROSTOV - DAY
The destination is the oldest cathedral in the Rostov
kremlin, the Cathedral of the Assumption, the 'Uspenski
Sobor', where Mariya Sidorova's coffin would be placed
for an overnight vigil attended by those close to her.

All of the mourners are lost in their thoughts as the
train rattles closer to the town of Rostov.

                                                        FADE OUT.

                                                        FADE TO:

EXT. THE SQUARE AT THE CATHEDRAL OF THE ASSUMPTION - DAY

The cortege enters the courtyard of the Cathedral, the
smallest of thirteen bells chimes from the arcaded
belfry. Grigor and Misha lead the pall-bearers.

                    MISHA (V.O.)
          The sight of the ancient
          Cathedral is a shock. The great
          churches of Russia have been
          neglected and left unmaintained
          by the Soviets. See how the
          cathedral walls are blotchy with
          neglect, the aspen wood roof
          shingles of the onion domes a
          dull dead grey, not like their
          usual silver silkiness. Mariya
          Sidorova will be turning in her
          grave.

                                                        CUT TO:

INT. THE CATHEDRAL OF THE ASSUMPTION - DAY

The cortege enters the cathedral. Grigor and Misha lead
the pall-bearers and place the coffin on a step in the
upper level of the sanctuary in front of the iconostasis.
A crowd of townsfolk have joined the mourners, and
assembling silently in the nave of the Cathedral. The
priest is lighting more candles and chants a short
service to receive the body of Mariya Sidorova into the
church.

                    MISHA (V.O.)
          We are invited to hold vigil
          until the following day, to
          commemorate the life of the
          deceased but of all the mourners
          only Grigor wants to remain for
          the night vigil. Although it is
          summer the interior of the
          Cathedral is cold, yet he
          insists that he was comfortable
          being wrapped only in a blanket.
          We are leaving him in a kneeling
          position in front of the coffin.
          I thought of remaining behind
          with my friend in reverence for
                    (MORE)

                    MISHA (CONT'D)
          Mariya Sidorova, who had always
          been hospitable and warm
          throughout our growing up years,
          like my own grandmother. But, I
          have decided that Grigor needs
          to be left to grieve in private,
          and so like the other mourners I
          will take leave of her.

                                        FADE TO:

INT. THE CATHEDRAL OF THE ASSUMPTION - DAY
The following morning.

                    MISHA (V.O.)
          We have found Grigor lying
          curled up alongside the
          coffin...his expression has
          changed as though the experience
          of his vigil has breathed a
          strange spirit into him.

                              ONE YEAR LATER

INT. A COFFEE BAR IN MOSCOW - DAY

Misha sits at a table waiting for Grigor, who arrives
late.

                    GRIGOR
               (hugs Misha)
          Hello, my friend, I'm late I
          know so my apologies.

                    MISHA
          Hey, you look older, more
          mature, maybe better-looking,
          even handsome...and your hair is
          well-cut. What is going on with
          you?

                    GRIGOR
          You guess.

                    MISHA
               (sees a ring on
                Grigor's finger)
          You're married!

                    GRIGOR
          Yes, Misha, for nearly a year
                    (MORE)

                    GRIGOR (CONT'D)
now, quietly and without fuss.
We invited no one, except my
parents and sister, and Ada's of
course. You see we were
expecting a baby, and had to
hurry up. There was nothing I
wanted more at that stage.

                    MISHA
My childhood friend, becoming a
father!

                    GRIGOR
Aah, but Misha, Ada had a
miscarriage and we lost the
baby. Of course she too was
devastated.

                    MISHA
          (touches Grigor's hand)
That is very sad news...my
condolences.

                    GRIGOR
Remember the Cathedral of the
Assumption at Rostov from where
my grandmother was buried...?

                    MISHA
          (nods)
How could I forget?

                    GRIGOR
Well, that night was a soulful
experience, and opened a clear
vista for me, in more ways than
one, which I...

                    MISHA
You seemed other-worldly and
mysterious the next morning. You
have never spoken of this before
to me, Grigor.

                    GRIGOR
Misha...what I am going to tell
you I haven't even shared with
Ada. She constantly scolds me,
because she says she doesn't
understand what is happening to
me and that is something which
is coming between us.

                    MISHA
          You make it sound as though you
          have done something terrible and
          can't help it. But I know you
          well enough to believe that
          nothing could ever make you do
          what you don't wish to do.

                                        INSERT:

INT. THE CATHEDRAL OF THE ASSUMPTION - DAY

The priest has committed Mariya Sidorova's body to the
Almighty. Six male singers, dressed in black form up on
the sanctuary and chant. Grigor leaves the mourners and
joins them.

                    MISHA (V.O.)
          The memory of him doing
          something untypical of him,
          flashes through my mind.
          Surprisingly, Grigor, who would
          never appear on a public
          platform has joined the line of
          singers and without having prior
          knowledge of the spiritual
          chants, he appears to be singing
          in complete harmony with the
          others.

                                        BACK TO:

INT. A COFFEE BAR IN MOSCOW - DAY

                    GRIGOR
          That night when I alone held
          vigil alongside my grandmother,
          Mariya Sidorova's coffin, I
          believed I experienced an
          epiphany...a manifestation of
          God. I have never mentioned this
          to anyone, but for some time
          before the funeral I felt
          possessed by a compulsion, which
          I could not understand. It was
          not physical, because I always
          felt fine, it was maybe what
          they call metaphysical. I now
          realise it was the prelude to my
          transformation into someone who
          is less diffident, more
          assertive, and more knowing
          about my destiny.

                    MISHA
          Which is?

                    GRIGOR
          I have to correct the wrongs
          which my family have suffered
          over the generations. My
          grandfather, Anatoly Danilovich
          Sidorov, because he was a White
          Russian, was shot by lesser
          mortals than himself, stripped
          of his family assets, his
          inheritance, and was forced to
          forget about his noble origins,
          just for the sake of a temporal
          political system.

Tears well in Grigor's eyes.

                    MISHA
          Tell me more about that
          epiphany, and how you knew what
          it was.

                    GRIGOR
          I lay on the floor after
          everyone had left me alone with
          the coffin in which lay my dear
          babushka, and studied the
          spiritual journeys expressed in
          those beautiful seventeenth-
          century frescoes, like those of
          Guri Nikitin up the walls and
          over the vaulted ceiling, then
          down again. Therein lay a
          enduring beauty of the artists'
          spirits, an outpouring of their
          souls to the glory of God, and
          therein lay my inspiration and I
          knew what I had to do. I was
          suddenly elevated from my state
          of mourning, knowing what was
          demanded of me. I had taken on
          the mantel of my family, and had
          gained strength and conviction.

                    MISHA
          What are you going to do?

                    GRIGOR
          I've completed my art training
          at the Academy and I have taken
          a job with the Department of Art
          Treasures.

                    MISHA
        But Grigor, a State job! Surely
        that's death for any one as
        creative and talented as you?
        What about your own painting?

                    GRIGOR
        First of all we need the money
        to buy an apartment, and there
        are not many jobs for a trained
        artist. Don't think that I'm
        wallowing in paperwork and stuck
        behind a desk. The job is much
        more 'hands on', as the saying
        goes. Since perestroika the
        government has embarked on huge
        restoration projects for the
        monasteries and cathedrals which
        the Soviets neglected. That's
        where I come in. I get to visit
        the sites from Pereslavl to
        Novgorod and even to St
        Petersburg, and write reports
        for the State funding. I spend
        as much time as I like with the
        artists and the craftsmen, many
        of them locals, and I share
        their passion for their work. It
        is premature, but one thing I
        can promise you at this stage,
        Misha, is that through my art, I
        shall be recovering from the
        past what is rightfully the
        heritage of the Sidorovs.

                    MISHA
        You speak in riddles, Grigor.
        Are you losing your mind. Come
        down to earth. Masha was not
        expecting you to become so
        obsessed with seeking
        restitution for the Sidorovs. In
        any case, it is insane and could
        be dangerous to try to reverse
        the course of history through
        inappropriate actions.

                                        DISSOLVE TO:

        EXT. THE WINTER PALACE SQUARE : ST PETERSBURG - DAY
        The scale of the Winter Palace is breathtaking with its
        two impressive frontages: one faces the enormous space of
        Palace Square, the other faces the Neva embankment.

Grigor stands transfixed before the sight of the Winter
Palace before him and meanders around the Square before
entering and then exiting onto the frontage facing the
Neva embankment.

EXT. THE NEVA EMBANKMENT OF THE WINTER PALACE - DAY
On the opposite bank is the Palace of Alexandr Menshikov,
the historic figure who has fired Grigor's imagination.

He reaches into his pocket and brings out the amber
cameo, inscribed with the Menshikov seal and rubs it as
though to coax out genie and bring history to life. He
returns it to his pocket.

A stranger, Dimitri, an older man, approaches quietly,
and his voice beside Grigor breaks into Grigor's
thoughts.

                    DIMITRI
               (offers his hand)
          Sir, I see you are a stranger
          here? Shall I tell you about St.
          Petersburg? It is a beautiful
          city, is it not? My name is
          Dimitri. I can tell you a lot
          about the Neva, and the history
          of this place.

                    GRIGOR
          I would be glad if you would. I
          am Grigor.

                    DIMITRI
          It will be my pleasure. Shall we
          sit here. Now, where shall I
          start? Well, it was at a time
          when Charles XII of Sweden was
          warmongering around the Baltic.
          At that stage Peter the Great
          was not accustomed to the
          strategies of war and suffered
          military setbacks. But Charles
          eventually blundered which gave
          the Tsar time to organise his
          forces and for the Russians to
          flex their muscles around the
          Gulf of Finland. Peter moved
          gradually closer to the estuary
          of the Neva river where it
          flowed into the Gulf and the
          Baltic. He himself then captured
          an important Swedish stronghold,
          so that by 1703 he could finally
          peg his claim to a windswept
                    (MORE)

                    DIMITRI (CONT'D)
          island on the Neva. There he
          built the Peter and Paul
          fortress, the staging post for
          his window on the world...his
          new city, St Petersburg. That's
          the fortress over there.

He points to the Peter and Paul fortress.

                    GRIGOR
          What do you know of Alexandr
          Menshikov?

                    DIMITRI
          Aah, I see you have former
          knowledge of a man close to
          Peter. Well, it seems that
          Alexandr Menshikov proved
          himself as a resourceful young
          man and with his successful
          cavalry raids under Peter's
          command, so he was elevated to
          the ranks of Prince and Field-
          Marshall. He became Tzar Peter's
          one-time favourite and his rise
          to favour led to the building of
          his own palace on Vasilievski
          island, over there.

He points to across the Neva river to the Palace.

                    DIMITRI (CONT'D)
          Such was his newfound wealth, he
          could afford to commission the
          Italian architect, Giovanni
          Fontana, to build for him that
          three-storeyed building with its
          own landing stage. Even large
          ships could berth opposite the
          front door.

                                          FLASHBACK:

EXT. THE NEVA EMBANKMENT ON VASILIEVSKI ISLAND - DAY
A misty image of Menshikov's Palace.

Construction of the building is underway, with tall-
masted ships alongside and activity on the embankment.

                    DIMITRI (V.O.)
          Menshikov had been commanded to
          build a university on that
          island, but he was wilful and
                    (MORE)

DIMITRI (CONT'D)
disobeyed. So, he earned the
wrath of the Tzar who had just
returned from another war.
Still, Menshikov rose so high up
in the ranks of the great nobles
that Pushkin, in one of his
poems, alluded to him as 'half
Tzar'. But his extravagance was
his eventual undoing, and to add
to his misdemeanours, he was
guilty of corruption. It was his
good fortune that the Tsar's
fondness for him probably
overcame his sense of justice
and he was warned for one last
time. Yet he went on to defraud
the government of one hundred
thousand roubles. Later,
however, when the two Greats,
Peter and Catherine, his patrons
at court were no longer there,
he was sent off into exile in
Siberia by the young Tzar, Peter
II.

                                    BACK TO:

EXT. THE NEVA EMBANKMENT OF THE WINTER PALACE - DAY

Dimitri rises from the seat.

            GRIGOR
That is a remarkable account of
someone who rose from nothing to
be recognised as a noble, and to
become the favourite of the
Tzar.

            DIMITRI
I see you are impressed, and
maybe too impressionable. It is
wise to keep a cool head. And
here, I am returning to you this
fine piece of amber. You see, my
good friend Grigor, beauty can
enchant you but is only a
veneer. Below the surface you
will find thieves waiting to rob
you of what is dear to you. This
beautiful seal I am certain is
of great value to you. Even
someone like me could remove it
from your pocket, because I spun
            (MORE)

                    DIMITRI (CONT'D)
          a yarn and distracted you. Take
          care, my good friend, St
          Petersburg is a scheming
          mistress! Here is your seal, and
          guard it with your life and may
          it bring you happiness. I bid
          you godspeed.

Grigor smiles, shakes his head, picks up his bag and
walks across to the ferry to the Peterhof Palace moored
alongside the embankment.

EXT. THE LANDING JETTY AT PETERHOF SUMMER PALACE - DAY
The Gulf of Finland itself is a boring flat stretch of
grey water, relieved only by Peter's bastion against
aggression, Kronstadt island, but the view up to the
Palace is breathtaking.

Grigor walks slowly towards the Palace as if in a trance.
Hundreds of visitors are moving around admiring the Grand
Cascade, a myriad of fountains playing at its foot with
the famous golden sculptures. The Samson sculpture in the
centre, is awash with water and sunlight. The sprays of
the fountains are mesmerising. Grigor takes the last
flight of steps to the Palace, where people congregate to
look across the canal towards the Gulf in the distance.
He goes to a side door and shows his official card and is
allowed entry to the Palace.

INT. THE ADMINISTRATION OFFICE OF THE PALACE - DAY

After a long wait, Grigor is assigned a secretary to take
him to the Office of the Curator. On the way they pass
the staff rooms and he takes a quick look at the sort of
people he would be working with every day. In one he says
a man reading a newspaper in a cloud of smoke. He is
shown into an office.

                    SECRETARY
          The acting Curator, Mr Yuri
          Stroganov, is busy at present,
          and will be with you shortly.
          The Curator himself is on sick
          leave for the next three months.

Grigor wanders around the room and to the window to look
over the gardens below.

                                        FADE TO:

The door opens and in walks Yuri Stroganov, the same man
who was smoking heavily and reading the newspaper.

                    STROGANOV
          (in Russian)
          *Dobro pozhalovat, Grigor Anatoly
          Sidorov. Kak pozhivaete?*

                    GRIGOR
          Spasibo khorosho!

                    STROGANOV
               (shows a seat)
          Pozhalusta.

Stroganov picks up the papers which Grigor has brought
with him. He studies them silently for some time.

                    STROGANOV (CONT'D)
          Is this your first visit to the
          Peterhof Palace?

                    GRIGOR
          Yes, and my first visit to St
          Petersburg, and so far I am
          bowled over.

                    STROGANOV
          What do you know of Peterhof and
          its restoration?

                    GRIGOR
          Well, I do know that the Palace
          was a casualty of the World Wars
          I and II, and what we now see is
          the restored version.

                    STROGANOV
          Yes, that is so. It was a great
          commitment by the Russian
          people, and the foresight of the
          State, to have restored it to
          what you see today, and may I
          say, individual families who
          have been patrons of the Arts
          over the centuries. I am proud
          to say the Stroganovs have done
          their duty to the country.
          We were wealthy merchants and
          commissioned Rastrelli to build
          a palace on Nevski Prospekt in
          the city. And the Stroganovs
          have been credited with opening
          up Siberia.

                    GRIGOR
          That is most impressive...

                    STROGANOV
          Now you're here to do some
          research for the Department of
          Art Treasures? I am right?

Grigor nods.

                    STROGANOV (CONT'D)
          Well, everything has got to go
          through me. I want a copy of
          your programme before you begin.
          Then we can discuss your modus
          operandi which has to fit with
          the culture and daily routine of
          the Palace. I shall be assigning
          to you someone who will report
          back to me.
          Now...

                    GRIGOR
          Of course, Sir.

                    STROGANOV
          I believe I should fill you in
          on a bit of history, like the
          wartime ravages to the Grand
          Palace and the later restoration
          work.

                    GRIGOR
          I would be glad if you would.

                    STROGANOV
          Well. it was turned into a
          museum in 1918, and during the
          Great Patriotic War of 1941 to
          1945 the Palace was burnt down,
          the Grand Cascade blown up, the
          Parks cut down and trenches dug.

                                        FLASHBACK TO:

EXT. THE GARDENS OF THE PETERHOF PALACE - DAY

A flashback to the time of World War II. The art
historians busy themselves securing the State treasures
of the Palace.

                    STROGANOV (V.O.)
          Eight thousand exhibits were
          evacuated in time, and fifty
          sculptures buried under the
          ground. So you see, Sidorov, the
          Russian people are clever, they
                    (MORE)

                         STROGANOV (V.O)(CONT'D)
            would never have allowed their
            treasures to fall into the hands
            of the enemy. Restoration
            started immediately following
            the War, and the Sampson
            Fountain, recreated by the
            sculptor Simonov, started
            functioning again in 1947...the
            first halls of the Palace opened
            to the public in 1954 while
            restoration work by a team of
            architects carried on. An
            offshoot of this amazing...

                                              FADE OUT.

                         STROGANOV
            So, you see Grigorovich Anatoly
            Sidorov...that's a very grand
            name, may I say...you will be
            joining a long line of
            restoration experts. I expect
            you to start tomorrow...

                         GRIGOR
            Tomorrow.

                         STROGANOV
            ...I shall see you promptly at
            ten o'clock, here, and will
            introduce the person who will be
            in charge of your day-to-day
            routine.

Stroganov points Grigor to the door.

INT. MISHA'S APARTMENT IN A SOVIET BLOCK - DAY

Misha sits at a table. A letter is pushed through the
letterbox. He picks it up and takes a seat. It is from
Grigor.

                         MISHA (V.O.)
                    (reads)
            "Dear Misha,hope that all goes
            well with you, my good friend. I
            have been in St Petersburg for a
            month now. Here, things couldn't
            be better and I have to pour out
            my heart to someone, and who
            better than to you? I am in
            love!"

                         MISHA
          So you're in love with St
          Petersburg. No, I'm wrong...!

                         MISHA (V.O.)
          "Her name is Lara. She is one of
          the junior curators at Peterhof,
          a New Age Russian girl, smart
          and sophisticated. But that is
          not all, first let me describe
          what makes her special. She is
          blonde, with the most perfect
          skin and blue eyes. I could
          paint her forever and ever. Her
          figure is perfect, and I cannot
          take my eyes off the sway of her
          hips, and fine legs. It is too
          much to put into words. How did
          we meet? Well, Stroganov, the
          acting curator - a typical *boyar*
          - introduced me to her as my
          facilitator, to assist me to
          carry out my work here. We both
          agree that Stroganov is a
          buffoon, and full of his own
          importance, but she has taught
          me how to handle him. He knows
          nothing about restoration and is
          a political appointment, a
          stand-in for the head curator
          who is on sick leave. But we
          humour him and make him feel
          that whatever decision is taken
          is his decision, and never show
          insurbordination! But I wander
          from what I really want to say.
          Lara is like a soul mate. We
          share the same love of fine art,
          and she often spends time with
          me on top of the scaffold
          admiring the paintings
          closeup"...

                                                      INSERT:

          INT. THE CHESMA HALL OF THE PALACE - DAY

          Grigor and Lara are on the mobile platform.

                         GRIGOR (O.C.)
          "You see, to get close-up for me
          to study the artist's technique,
          brushwork and pigmentation for
                         (MORE)

                    GRIGOR (CONT'D)
my assignment, it is essential
to be on a raised platform. It
is on wheels, and we move it
around to view the paintings.
Visitors are still able to walk
around it and they do so
throughout the day. But after
the Palace has closed in the
evening, Lara and I have the
place to ourselves. She has keys
and the security code so we can
come and go as we please. That
is where it all started! We'd
only known each other for two
weeks, when one evening we
stayed late, the low sun was
casting a magical glow through
the north windows into the
Chesma Hall where the enormous
canvases of sea battles are
exhibited. The soft light
illuminated the rich sensual
colours and textures of the
paintings. We were enchanted,
and I felt her hand reach for
mine...and things took over
completely from there. I was
powerless to resist her and we
made love on top of the scaffold
in that romantic setting so
beloved by both of us. We never
gave a thought as to what the
ghosts of Peter the Great or
Catherine would have thought of
that...when last had anyone made
love in that Palace?!"

                                    BACK TO:

INT. MISHA'S APARTMENT IN A SOVIET BLOCK - DAY

                    MISHA
          Indeed my friend!
             (reads on)

                    GRIGOR (O.C.)
"I think that Stroganov is
always suspicious about what
might happen behind his back, as
he can see the chemistry between
us. In his presence we behave
impeccably, almost subservient,
but he has a nose for anything
             (MORE)

                    GRIGOR (O.C.)(CONT'D)
which is out of routine, even
the protocol in relationships.
It will be devastating for Ada
to know about this, and in time
I shall have to tell her. We
have not been enjoying the same
relationship as when we got
married, which is partly my
fault. I have sometimes been
distant and don't communicate
just to avoid a confrontation. I
know that it is a man's way,
where women verbalise what they
are concerned about or not happy
with. It sometimes drove me out
of the apartment rather than to
respond to her...I am a pig! I
beg you not to mention anything
about Lara to her, Misha, my
dear friend."

                    MISHA
You ask too much, Grigor. How
can I give you my unconditional
support, my wayward friend?

INT. THE CHESMA HALL IN THE PETERHOF PALACE

Grigor sits cross-legged on a mobile scaffold studying
the paintings of the Russian naval victory over the Turks
in the Battle Chesma of 1770. With him is Lara who reads
from notes.

                    GRIGOR
           For the quality of the imagery,
           it is strange that some
           historians criticise Jacob
           Philipp Hackert for not showing
           more realism in these paintings.

                    LARA
           Yes. To assist the artist,
           Catherine II even arranged for a
           frigate to be blown up in the
           harbour of Livorno Italy.

                    GRIGOR
           All credit to him then for
           having captured the exploding
           ships, fires on board, smoke and
           fireballs with such dramatic
           effect.

He works in silence for a while.

                    LARA
         These are national treasures. I
         hope you agree that your report
         to the Academy should emphasise
         that. So often its members spend
         their time fighting amongst
         themselves and the artifacts get
         forgotten.

                    GRIGOR
         I rate them very highly. On the
         quality of the brush strokes
         alone they are masterpieces.

The acting curator Stroganov enters and wanders around
the scaffold.

                    STROGANOV
         Look, Sidorov, I have just had
         another phone call from the
         Department Head in Moscow. You
         have exceeded your allotted time
         and I am being blamed for
         overrunning the budget. How much
         longer are you going to be?

                    GRIGOR
         I am nearly finished with the
         Chesma hall, Sir, and will be
         going to the Rotari Room
         tomorrow.

                    STROGANOV
         See that you do. And Lara, I
         think you are spending far too
         much time on that scaffold, you
         are a distraction.

Grigor and Lara look at each other and give a knowing
smile.

                    LARA
         Grigor needs someone to take
         notes which will be sent to the
         Department, Sir. I have to
         ensure they follow the
         Department's own form.

Stroganov leaves, not entirely convinced.

                                        FADE OUT.

                                        FADE TO:

INT. THE ROTARI ROOM OF THE PETERHOF PALACE - DAY

The Rotari Room, or the Cabinet of Modes and Graces as it was sometimes called, is the next room into which the scaffold is moved. Of all the halls of the Palace, it is perhaps the most unusual, as it breaks with the tradition. Grigor is on the mobile scaffold and Lara studies the portraits below.

> LARA
> Not only are they of exceptional quality, but each must be a portrait of a person, not just of a convenient subject, who posed for the artist at the time. They differ in appearance and even age.

> GRIGOR
> An incredible work...three hundred and sixty-eight paintings of young women. And, all still in a single collection. They were bought from Rotari's widow in 1764 and have been kept together ever since.

Lara gets onto the scaffold and reads from some notes.

> LARA
> "Peter the Great was determined to bring the Russian people closer to the sophisticated cultures of the West. His influence was so compelling that even after his death, instead of icons, the walls of the Rotari Room are covered with portraits of ordinary young women. It says here that they convey a symbolic message that Russia at the time aspired to the manner of the outside world in the fine arts."

> GRIGOR
> That's a neat summation. Whoever made that interpretation knows the history of the Russian culture as expressed through its fine art.

> LARA
> Grigor.

> GRIGOR
> Yes?

                    LARA
          Let's do something else tonight,
          go to a movie or concert. You
          deserve a break from fine art.

                    GRIGOR
          I don't think so. The Department
          head already wants my head for
          taking so long. I have to work
          again after hours tonight.

                    LARA
          The Department will never let
          you go.

                    GRIGOR
          Are you missing me?

He jumps off the scaffold and goes up close to her, and
pecks her on the cheek.

                    LARA
          Don't flatter yourself, Sidorov!

They both laugh.

INT. ARCHIVE ROOM OF THE PETERHOF PALACE - NIGHT
Lara and the staff had finally left Grigor alone in the
Palace. He feels compelled to continue with his work,
driven by the desire to know more about Rotari's legacy.

                    GRIGOR (V.O.)
               What's this?

He opens a leather portmanteau wrapped with string and
marked "P.Rotari"

                    GRIGOR (V.O.)
               P.Rotari.

He removes a box which has the artist's crest on the lid
and trawls through the documents written in cyrillic.

                    GRIGOR (V.O.)
                 (with mounting
                  anticipation)
          Names of women who posed for
          him? Dates of their sittings?
          How many roubles he paid them?
          More dates? Addresses?

He reads down the list.

> GRIGOR (O.C.)
> "Menshikova - Tatyana, daughter
> of Aleksandr Danilovich
> Menshikov, 5 November 1725,
> Vasilievski island, St
> Petersburg. 1 rouble x 4 (signed
> P.R)!" Must be for four
> paintings.

Grigor's breathing becomes laboured as though an invisible force has tightened around his chest.

> GRIGOR (O.C.) (CONT'D)
> This is a revelation...

He lies down on the floor and stares at the ceiling.

> GRIGOR (O.C.) (CONT'D)
> Some psychic power has led me to
> this room, these documents, to
> Tatyana.

He stands and with shaking hands returns the fragile yellowed documents to the box. Then finds another with a pencilled grid with writing in each block and resembling the layout of the room.

> GRIGOR (O.C.)(CONT'D)
> Aha, the layout of the paintings
> on the walls, with the names of
> the subjects.

He scans down the names.

> GRIGOR (O.C)(CONT'D)
> Just as I was hoping...here she
> is mentioned in four places, "T.
> Menshikov".

He makes a quick copy of the grid.

INT. THE ROTARI ROOM OF THE PETERHOF PALACE - NIGHT

Grigor walks through the darkened galleries of the Palace with his torch. In the Rotari room on and off the scaffold he quickly locates each of the four paintings.

> GRIGOR (O.C.)
> Tatyana! From close-up she
> resembles no other portrait,
> except the others of herself, a
> tribute to Pietro Rotari's
> exceptional skill as a portrait
> artist.

Tears well up in his eyes.

                    GRIGOR (O.C.)(CONT'D)
          The beautiful daughter of
          Aleksandr Danilovich Menshikov.
          Am I on the right path, Masha?

                                        FADE OUT:

                                        FADE TO:

EXT. THE EAGLE GATES TO ALEXANDER GARDENS, MOSCOW - DAY

It is a sunny afternoon and large beds of tulips stand
tall in their glorious rich monotones, swaying slightly
in the breeze. Misha revels in the heat of the sun,
unconcerned about having to wait for Grigor who is late.
Grigor arrives dressed formally, they hug in greeting,
then start to stroll, Grigor with his arm on Misha's
shoulder.

                    MISHA
          I got your message at my work to
          meet here. You said you had
          something urgent to tell me.

                    GRIGOR
          Misha, I am in love.

                    MISHA
          Now you're confusing me Grigor,
          my friend. Why are you telling
          me this again, and what's so
          urgent. Is it the same girl?

                    GRIGOR
          You mean Lara. Yes, of course I
          love her, but don't be so
          pedestrian, Misha! Being 'in
          love' need not always mean with
          another person...one can be in
          love with something spiritually
          important, something with deep
          associations, something
          beautiful, something which can
          change your life...

                    MISHA
          I am always suspicious of your
          extreme emotional attachments,
          Grigor. You are as fickle as the
          wind.

Grigor's expression is other-worldly, of happiness which
he urgently wants to share.

                    GRIGOR
          When you hear what I have to
          tell you, you will also
          understand how such a 'Damascus'
          experience has changed my reason
          for living.

The reach the Tzarina Gate into the Kremlin. They queue
with many others wanting to enter the Kremlin. Grigor is
pulled aside by a security guard and frisked.

                    MISHA (V.O.)
          I later recall this incident and
          change my prejudice about the
          power of psychic assocations.

They pass through the gate and into the Kremlin precinct.

EXT. INSIDE THE KREMLIN PRECINCT - DAY

                    GRIGOR
          Let me tell you more about the
          work I've been doing at
          Peterhof, and its importance to
          my career with the Department of
          Art Treasures. It was in the
          Rotari Room that the pieces
          started coming together for me
          through the 'Damascus'
          experience. You see it's Tatyana
          who's my new love, Misha.

                    MISHA
          Tatyana? What happened to Lara?

                    GRIGOR
          No, Misha, there are four
          portraits of Tatyana in the
          Rotari Room. She is the only
          true likeness we have of a
          Menshikov, and a beautiful one
          at that. I want to paint copies
          of those four paintings of
          her...

                    MISHA
          That's bizarre, Grigor. They are
          just likenesses and over four
          hundred years old at that?

                        GRIGOR
            The work is so realistic as to
            almost achieve a photographic
            record of a girl in the prime of
            her youth. I am compelled to do
            it, Misha.

They reach Cathedral Square, and hear a male choir
singing inside the Cathedral of the Dormition. They enter
with others to listen to the glorious pageant of sound in
the frescoed interior under the vaulted roof.

INT. THE CATHEDRAL OF THE DORMITION - DAY
The soaring iconostasis in the sacristy and the passion
of the singers is uplifting.

Grigor and Misha stand silently for a while, then exit
the Cathedral.

EXT. THE KREMLIN PRECINCT - DAY

They walk for some distance through the landscaped
precinct of the Kremlin then Grigor breaks the silence.

                        GRIGOR
            Ada and I are going away
            together. We haven't been
            getting along too well of late.
            She accuses me of not loving her
            and loving my work more. I know
            she's right. We thought it might
            help if I got right away from
            the workplace, and we could try
            to restore the spark in our
            relationship. She says I have
            manic mood swings, Misha, which
            she can't deal with.

                        MISHA
            She could be right, my friend.

They stroll sharing the pleasure of their friendship and
admire the architecture as the walk.

                        MISHA (V.O.) (CONT'D)
            It is true that Grigor is a
            slave to his vivid imagination,
            but I suspect that there were
            more underlying causes for his
            manic state. He embraces life
            more passionately than most, his
            enthusiasm for his art
            outstripping the normal, but
                        (MORE)

                    MISHA (V.O.)(CONT'D)
          depression is not a symptom I
          have observed in him right from
          our childhood. Falling easily in
          love is Grigor's weakness, but
          again that does not confirm any
          incipient disorder.

                                                  FADE OUT.

INT. THE ROTARI ROOM IN THE PETERHOF PALACE - NIGHT
It is after hours and the Palace is in darkness. Grigor
is on the scaffold with two lights trained onto one of
Tatyana's portraits.

With a magnifying glass Grigor studies the canvas close-
up to capture a detailed impression of the colours and
the tonal nuances with which artist Pietro Rotari had
brought Tatyana's image to life.

                    GRIGOR (O.C.)
          Hold that pose, Tatyana, while I
          capture your beauty. If Lara
          knew I was here with you she
          might become jealous. She has
          been asking why I am spending so
          much time in this room. Ahaa, I
          detect a slight blush on your
          cheeks.

He paints.

                    GRIGOR (O.C.) (CONT'D)
          Of course I always make it up to
          Lara, and she is loving and
          forgiving. But I have to follow
          what my beloved *babushka*
          assigned to me. Remember Masha's
          last written words were to me?
          She said: "Of all the Sidorovs,
          you are the one who can carry
          the name forward and uphold and
          restore its dignity after the
          sacrifices of your forebears.
          The family has its roots in
          history and as you know was
          stripped of its dignity...". She
          often called me 'Grigor the
          Great'.

He paints with tears rolling down his cheeks.

                    GRIGOR (O.C.)
          Masha, am I doing enough? Will
                    (MORE)

                    GRIGOR (O.C.)(CONT'D)
          copies of these original
          paintings of Tatyana Menshikov
          be enough to restore that
          dignity and the family's noble
          heritage? Will only replicas be
          enough?

Grigor puts down his paints and sobs.

                                        FADE TO:

INT. THE ROTARI ROOM IN THE PETERHOF PALACE - DUSK
The Palace staff have gone home, and Grigor is using the
evening to continue painting his replicas of Tatyana.

Stroganov, the curator enters the Rotari Room and
surprises Grigor on the scaffold. Grigor hides his
canvas, and picks up his notes.

                    STROGANOV
          Sidorov, what is this? Working
          overtime? You haven't cleared
          this with me. I shall have to
          include this oversight in my
          report to the Department unless
          you have a good explanation.

                    GRIGOR
               (startled)
          Mr Stroganov, you see Sir, I am
          behind with my work as the
          Department laid down the time to
          be spent and it is impossible to
          complete my assignment in that
          time.

                    STROGANOV
          Well, I could make an exception.
          However, it would depend.

                    GRIGOR
          Depend?

                    STROGANOV
          On you undertaking an assignment
          for me. My granddaughter is
          getting married and I have sung
          your praises so highly that she
          insists that my present to her
          should be a Grigor Sidorov
          painting.

                    GRIGOR
          (relieved)
          Of course, Sir, of course...

                    STROGANOV
          She would like a watercolour
          depiction of the Grand Cascade.
          You could use some of the late
          afternoon hours, Sidorov,
          instead of being stuck up there
          on the scaffold.

                    GRIGOR
          It will be my pleasure.

                                        DISSOLVE TO:

EXT. THE GRAND CASCADE OF THE PETERHOF PALACE - DAY

Grigor works on an easel developing the painting of the
magical fountains, waterfalls grottoes and gold
sculptures for Stroganov's granddaughter. Visitors to the
Palace gather to watch as he paints. It is dusk when Lara
approaches and Grigor is alone and still working.

                    LARA
              (hugs Grigor from
              behind)
          Will you also paint one for me,
          and not just for strange women
          who make demands on you?

Grigor puts his brushes aside, turns and hugs her.

                    GRIGOR
          I only waste my talents on
          strange woman. How strange can
          you be?

                    LARA
              (leads him away)
          Let me show you.

They head for the forest, holding hands, then play
amongst the trees, hug and kiss. Lara leads the way to a
grotto under a waterfall. They get soaked, kiss, then
start undressing before making love. They lie drenched
but close.

                    GRIGOR
          You do know that I've been told
          by the Department to leave
          Peterhof as they have other work
          for me?

                    LARA
          I'm going with you.

                    GRIGOR
          What about your work?

                    LARA
          I can't stay here without you,
          Grigor. You are part of me now.

                                        FADE OUT.

                                        FADE TO:

INT. STAFF QUARTERS IN THE PETERHOF PALACE - NIGHT

Grigor stows his four paintings in a red canister, and is
surprised by the staff who gather to wish him resounding
farewell.

                    STROGANOV
          On behalf of the staff, Sidorov,
          we are sorry that are leaving.
          But, alas, the needs of the
          Department of Art Treasures come
          first. Perhaps you will be back
          again one day.

                    LARA
          Grigor, we have a present for
          you. It is a limited edition of
          the art collection in the
          Palace. It's a memento so that
          you will remember us all and the
          art treasures you are leaving
          behind.

Grigor accepts the book, opens it and reads.

                    GRIGOR
          "To Grigor Anatoly Sidorov,
          esteemed Artist, Authority and
          Curator of Russian Art Heritage,
          from his Associates in the
          Summer Palace of Peter the
          Great, Peterhof, St Petersburg,
          Russia." Wow, I'm overwhelmed.
          Thank you one and all.

He kisses Lara on each cheek. Although formal, there is
familiarity and the staff have noticed the chemistry
between them.

                    STAFF
               (sing)
          Yah,yah,yah!

INT. THE ST PETERSBURG PULKOVO AIRPORT TERMINAL - DAY

Grigor finds a seat, sits and waits. There is little else
to do but ponder about the lives of his fellow
travellers, each living in a private coccoon and
remaining strangers to one another. His flight is
announced and he rushes forward to join the quickforming
queue. It moves forward very slowly. Grigor hands his
ticket to the airline ticket clerk, a country girl with
too much make-up. She flashes her heavy black lashes at
him.

                    TICKET CLERK
          You travel by air a lot, mister
          Grigor... Sidorov. How do you
          spend your time in St
          Petersburg? Alone?

                    GRIGOR
          Sometimes...

                    TICKET CLERK
          (hands back his ticket)
          Well, I can change all that.

                    GRIGOR
          I have girlfriend.

                    TICKET CLERK
          Lucky girl. That's a pity. Go
          through to the departure lounge.
          Next.

                                        FADE OUT:

                                        A MONTH LATER:

INT. MISHA'S APARTMENT IN A SOVIET BLOCK - DAY

The phone rings. It is Lara on an assignment and phoning
from Moscow.

                    LARA
          Mikhail, we haven't met, but you
          might know about me. I am Lara,
          Grigor's friend from Peterhof.

                    MISHA
          Of course, Grigor has spoken
          about you. How is he...?

Prolonged silence.

                    LARA
               (tearful)
          He's not well...he is at the
          dacha in Kolomenskoye, and I am
          here in Moscow on an assignment.
          I wanted to stay with him, but
          have to return to St Petersburg.

                    MISHA
          What seems to be the matter?

                    LARA
          Please try and go to
          Kolomenskoye as soon as you can.
          He needs you, his closest
          friend. I can't bear it when he
          is unhappy. He might do
          something unthinkable to
          himself, but I have to leave for
          St Petersburg without delay.

                    MISHA
               (looks at the calendar)
          My weekend is clear and I will
          then have to time to go to the
          dacha.

                    LARA
          You're a good friend, Misha.
          Please let me know about...

                    MISHA
          I will, of course.

                    MISHA (V.O.)
          A pity that Lara has to go back
          to St Petersburg. I have heard
          so much about her and I want to
          meet her, the girl who has
          stolen Grigor's heart. Or is it
          Tatyana of the four portraits?

                                   FADE TO:

EXT. A FOREST ROAD IN KOLOMENSKOYE - DAY

Misha is on a bicycle borrowed from the station master.
He rides to the Mariya's Sidorova's dacha through the
birch forest to a cluster of similar traditional dachas.

EXT. OUTSIDE MARIYA SIDOROVA'S DACHA - DAY
Grigor wears an artist's smock and is barefoot. His hair
has grown down to his shoulders.

Misha reaches the dacha and finds Grigor on a ladder
painting the window surround in bizarre colours. Grigor
waves when he sees him and descends from the ladder.

                    GRIGOR
               (hugs Misha)
          I was touching up the old girl
          so that she doesn't feel
          neglected.

                    MISHA
          My friend, you have lost weight.

                    GRIGOR
          I've been working too hard.

They walk to the door of the dacha.

INT. MARIYA SIDOROVA'S DACHA - DAY

                    MISHA
          I haven't been inside for years,
          Grigor. It is just as your
          beloved *babushka* left it, except
          more untidy!

Grigor ignores the attempt at levity.

                    MISHA (V.O.)
          His eyes are misty and there is
          none of his usual levity in his
          greeting.

                    MISHA
          I remember so well that stove
          where we warmed ourselves during
          those cold winter nights. And
          there is the bench at the table
          where we sat and listened to the
          adults talking, not knowing what
          they were saying half the time.

Grigor puts on the kettle.

                    GRIGOR
          I knew most of the time. They
          were talking about how the
          family had suffered at the hands
          of the Bolsheviks, stripped of
          their possession, our heritage
          and our lineage.

                         MISHA
               You have to move on, Grigor.

                         GRIGOR
               I tried to when I married Ava.
               But she has divorced me now on
               the grounds that I was
               preoccupied with my family's so-
               called noble connections,
               something I never stopped
               talking about.

                         MISHA
               I am sorry.

                         GRIGOR
               Then she scorned my claim that
               what really belonged to my
               family was in State galleries
               around the country was a
               childhood dream, and that it
               meant more to me than anything
               else. What could I do, Misha? I
               could never confide my innermost
               thoughts to her, in case she
               became an accessory to what I
               had in mind.

                         MISHA
               Just what did you have in mind,
               Grigor?

                         GRIGOR
               They are hanging on the wall
               over there. Those are four
               paintings of Tatyana, my copies
               from the Rotari portraits in the
               Peterhof Palace. They remind me
               of happy times at Peterhof.

                         MISHA
               Is that all. Why would Ada
               become an accessory for
               something that artists do. You
               could say it was part of your
               work. No, Grigor, you had
               nothing to worry about.

Misha goes close up to paintings as Grigor goes to make
the tea.

                         MISHA (CONT'D)
               There is no doubting your
               talent, my friend. These are
                         (MORE)

                    MISHA (CONT'D)
          indeed the finest portraits I
          have ever seen in my infrequent
          forays to art galleries.

They sit and drink tea.

                    MISHA (CONT'D)
          Lara phoned me. She was worried
          about you, Grigor. And, she said
          the Department has been upset
          with you.

                    GRIGOR
          I've been sacked?

                    MISHA
          No! Why?

                    GRIGOR
          Because they say I spent more
          time than was budgeted for the
          Peterhof job. And because they
          don't understand, Misha.
          Painting is to the artist like
          his or her lifeblood. You can't
          make rules for artists, they
          function almost as though driven
          by an invisible force. And, you
          have to respond to that force,
          otherwise you can even get sick.

                    MISHA
          Yes, but there are budgets...

Pause.

                    GRIGOR
          So you like Tatyana? She's an
          inspiration and I have great
          plans for her.

                    MISHA
          What could you mean?

                    GRIGOR
          Well, you see, she really does
          belong in the Peterhof palace,
          but I have other plans for her.

                    MISHA
          Now you've lost me.

                    GRIGOR
          Misha, please stay the night. It
          will be like old times. We can
          drink some vodka together.

                    MISHA
          I'll stay but it's getting cold
          in here. I'll fetch some wood.

                                        FADE OUT:

                                        FADE TO:

INT. MARIYA SIDOROVA'S DACHA - NIGHT

Grigor and Misha sit eating and drinking at the table in
convivial conversation.

                    MISHA (V.O.)
          As we eat, I watch as Grigor
          recovers some of his
          conviviality. We talk about
          everything under the sun, and I
          allow myself to be lulled into
          believing that my worries, and
          those of Lara, are unfounded.
          Grigor will survive, in his own
          way. Who were we to prescribe
          how he should live his life?

                                        DISSOLVE:

EXT. A STREET ALONG THE FONTANKA CANAL ST PETERSBURG -
DAY

Grigor emerges from the metro and walks in the street
alongside the canal. The buildings along the embankment
were all three storeys high, with facades similar in
their fenestration and classical style elements. He
passes a large well-tended garden with an arboretum laid
out behind tall black iron railings. Further behind, and
just visible, is a mansion of fine proportions and
interesting turreting, no doubt the house of a nobleman.
He stands there for sometime, absorbing the scene.

                                        INSERT:

EXT. AT THE GATES OF THE MANSION WITH THE ARBORETUM - DAY

An imagined picture of his grandfather Anatoly as a
child, playing in that beautiful garden, occupies
Grigor's mind. His parents sit under umbrellas on the

lawn and are brought tea by servants. Grigor lingers. A group of Bolsheviks on horseback suddenly appear out of nowhere and throw over the table and chairs and scatter the occupants, cruelly ending the stylish culture of high sophistication.

                                        BACK TO:

EXT. AT THE GATES OF THE MANSION WITH THE ARBORETUM - DAY

A gardener walks towards the iron railings where Grigor is standing, to enquire about his interest in the place, but Grigor moves quickly away. Before he leaves he notices a cast iron shield within the elaborate design of the gate which bears the name of the occupant: "A. Danilovich". He removes the amber seal and looks at the inscription - Danilovich was a Menshikov family name. He strolls on in a state of levitation as he progresses along the canal.

                                        DISSOLVE:

INT. STADIUM WITH ROCK CONCERT TAKING PLACE - NIGHT

Grigor and Lara are amongst the crowds of screaming fans at the end of a rock concert. They leave with a stream of people heading for the exits.

INT. LARA'S APARTMENT ST PETERSBURG - MAGIC

Grigor and Lara, burst into her apartment and immediately start to undress and make love. After sex they linger under the covers.

                    LARA
          I love you Grigor Sidorov.

                    GRIGOR
          Say no more!

                    LARA
          You are your old self.

                    GRIGOR
          I'm hungry.

                    LARA
          I hope only for food!

                    GRIGOR
          Come here...!

Lara jumps out of bed.

                    LARA
          I'll heat up the *borsch*, and I
          have some bread.

Grigor and Lara sit at the table, eat and converse.

                    GRIGOR
          I have something to tell you,
          which you might not like to
          hear.

                    LARA
          You are so mysterious,
          Grigorishki. What is it?

                    GRIGOR
          I've been sacked by the
          Department.

                    LARA
          No!

                    GRIGOR
          Spending more than the allotted
          time to the task.

                    LARA
          But you slaved away on top of
          that scaffold, that is as long
          as I left you alone...

                    GRIGOR
          I wasn't doing the Department's
          work. I was making copies of
          Rotari's portraints of Tatyana
          Menshikov. There were four of
          them.

                    LARA
          You old fox!

                    GRIGOR
          But, you might not approve of
          the real plan and I also know
          that no one would ever know if
          my four paintings of Tatyana are
          put in place of those of the
          artist Pietro Rotari. That is
          what I am going to do.

                    LARA
          You can't do that, those are
          State treasures!

                    GRIGOR
Please, Lara, try to understand.
It matters a lot to my well-
being to complete what I have
started. It is a task which my
family, my *babushka*, has
bestowed on me and I must
fulfill it. For my family's
losses the compensation would be
symbolic. Possession of the four
paintings of one of our
ancestors, would be small
compensation for being stripped
of our property after the
Bolshevik revolution.

                    LARA
I am beginning to wonder what
sort of person I am in love
with.

                    GRIGOR
Lara please.

                    LARA
I have to ask myself, must I
confine my love to your masterly
skill with the paint brush and
passion for fine art, or can I
love the whole person who is a
thief, with no care about the
implications should he get
caught?

                    GRIGOR
I won't be caught. I have an
accomplice.

                    LARA
And who would that be?

                    GRIGOR
His name is Vovo.

                    LARA
    (laughs)
Vovo? Who the hell is Vovo?

                    GRIGOR
He is a pickpocket, a master at
sleight of hand.

                    LARA
Grigor, are you serious?

                    GRIGOR
          I was travelling on the metro
          after I boarded a metro train at
          Nevsky Prospekt and he opened
          the canister with my paintings
          and removed them without me
          knowing. Vovo earned a few slaps
          to the head for his trouble. I
          threatened to take him to police
          station, then didn't because he
          pleaded as he was already on
          police records. Instead I asked
          him to be my accomplice.

                    LARA
          You are mad, Grigor. He's a
          petty thief and could expose the
          whole plan to win favour with
          the authorities.

                    GRIGOR
          I have faith in his ability to
          help me pull this off.

Pause

                    GRIGOR (CONT'D)
          You've said my work is as good
          as the old masters. We would be
          the only persons in the whole
          wide world to know.

                    LARA
          Including Vovo, the pickpocket.
          I ask myself, must I be content
          to become an accessory, because,
          unless I report you to the
          Department that is what I will
          be.

                                        FADE OUT.

                                        FADE TO:

EXT. DECEMBRIST SQUARE ST PETERSBURG - DAY

In the background is the golden dome of St Isaac
cathedral. Grigor sits on a park bench talking to himself
while waiting to meet with Vovo. He has the red canister
next to him on the bench.

                    GRIGOR (O.S.)
          It was difficult to persuade
                    (MORE)

                    GRIGOR (CONT'D)
          Lara. She was right, it is
          risky, but said she couldn't
          stand in my way. The keys to her
          locker and the keys and security
          code to the staff entrance at
          Peterhof will make the job
          easier.

Unbeknown to Grigor Vovo walks up behind him, then turns
and sits down next to him.

                    VOVO
          Remember me?

                    GRIGOR
          You rascal, how could I forget
          you.

                    VOVO
            (grins)
          Before I forget here is what I
          found in your pocket.

                    GRIGOR
          That, my friend, deserves a good
          hiding. Now you owe me a second
          time.

                    VOVO
          What do you want from me?

                    GRIGOR
          You are going to help me to
          recover what rightfully belongs
          to my family...

                                        FADE OUT.

                                        FADE TO:

EXT. THE GARDENS OF THE PETERHOF PALACE - NIGHT

Grigor emerges from a gazebo at nightfall and gives three
low whistles. A moment later Vovo emerges from the
forest. Together they move silently towards the Palace.
They remain in the shadows of the floodlights to reach
the staff entrance. Working in the semidark, Grigor gains
entry for them using Lara's keys and the security code.

INT. STAFF LOCKER ROOMS OF THE PETERHOF PALACE - NIGHT

Grigor goes to Lara's locker which he opens with a key and stows the red canister with his replica paintings there. He and Vovo enter the rooms of the Palace in the dark. Grigor leads them straight to the Rotari Room.

INT. THE SECURITY OFFICE OF THE PETERHOF PALACE - NIGHT

The alarm has been activated in the security office and shows a flickering light. The security guard Sergei Demidovsky is roused from his slumber. He jumps to attention, grabs his overcoat, torch and truncheon and races outside into the night. He shines his torch into the shadows and sees nothing. He then notices a flickering light from a window upstairs, and rushes back to phone the Curator, who is working late in a separate part of the Palace.

                    DEMIDOVSKY
          (excited)
          Sir...

                    STROGANOV
          What is it, Demidovsky? Why do
          you bother me?

                    DEMIDOVSKY
          Sir, sir, the alarm has gone
          off, and, and I've seen flashes
          of light from one of the
          upstairs windows.

                    STROGANOV
          Calm yourself. Where upstairs?

                    DEMIDOVSKY
          I'm not sure, Sir, but I think
          we'll soon locate the room.

                    STROGANOV
          No one has permission to be in
          the Palace tonight. An intruder
          wouldn't know that the alarm has
          been activated...am I right,
          Demidovsky?

                    DEMIDOVSKY
          It's a silent alarm, Sir. No,
          they wouldn't know.

                    STROGANOV
          (smiles)
          Good. Go ahead, Demidovsky, I'll
          meet you at the staircase. Don't
          use your flashlight, nor turn on
          any lights.

INT. THE GRAND STAIR PETERHOF PALACE - NIGHT

They meet at the grand stair and take the steps two at a
time to reach the upper floor in silence.

                                            CUT TO:

INT. INTERLEADING ROOMS OF THE PALACE - NIGHT

Stroganov and Demidovsky move through the first few rooms
until they are able to look down along the length of the
Palace down through the interleading doorways. An
intermittent flashing light draws their attention, and
Stroganov takes the lead, first peering into each room
before proceeding. They notice that it comes from the
Rotari Room and hear the sound of voices. Stroganov
enters the room and switches on his torch.

INT. THE ROTARI ROOM PETERHOF PALACE - NIGHT

Vovo, as yet a stranger, sits astride the shoulders of
Grigor. Both hold torches while studying the paintings in
the top row. The two freeze as they stare into the beams
of the flashlights. Vovo recovers first and slides down
off Grigor's shoulders and hides behind him, shocked by
their discovery.

                    STROGANOV
          What the...? Is that you
          Sidorov?

Demidovsky rushes forward and grabs Grigor around the
neck in a vice grip.

                    STROGANOV (CONT'D)
          Sidorov, Sidorov, Sidorov, what
          do you think you're doing?

                    GRIGOR
          I...

                    STROGANOV
          You have no business to be in
          the Palace, day or night. Your
          assignment is complete. What is
          the meaning of this intrusion?

                    GRIGOR
          I..., I was showing my friend
          the work of Pietro Rotari.

                         STROGANOV
          Preposterous, Sidorov. Do you
          think that explanation is going
          to help the case against you? I
          have to report this to the
          police, and you will be facing a
          criminal charge for breaking
          into and entering a State
          treasury, and exposing its
          heritage collections to
          unauthorised persions, and
          what's more after hours when
          there is no surveillance. Who is
          this...this... with you?

                         GRIGOR
          His name is Vovo.

Grigor is released from Demidovsky's grip and he pushes
Vovo forward to show his face.

                         STROGANOV
          How did you get in to the Palace
          without my authority?

Grigor remains silent.

                         STROGANOV (CONT'D)
          Right, so I suppose you think
          you might be worsening your
          case. Take these two back to the
          security office, Demidovsky, and
          I'll call the police.

INT. THE SECURITY OFFICE OF THE PETERHOF PALACE - NIGHT

The security buzzer and the red light are still
flickering. Demidovsky turns off the alarm.

                         STROGANOV
          You didn't know, Sidorov, that
          the Palace's internal alarm
          system is silent, except here in
          the security office.

Grigor shakes his head.

                         STROGANOV (CONT'D)
          Let this be a lesson to you. The
          Palace has two alarm systems,
          one on entering after hours,
          which is audible, and another
          which detects movement inside
          the Palace and is silent. If you
                            (MORE)

had authorisation to be in the
Palace, Demidovsky here would
have to deactivate the internal
alarm. But you did not have
authorisation and so you see,
the system has done its job
well.

Stroganov turns to Demidovsky.

                    STROGANOV (CONT'D)
          You keep an eye on these two,
          while I phone the local police.

Stroganov leaves.

                    DEMIDOVSKY
          Yes, Sir.

Demidovsky seems unsure of himself, but makes the two
intruders sit back to back on the floor and ties their
hands together. He goes to sit at his desk, opens a
drawer, takes out a cigarette and lights up. He tilts
back his chair and, with a look of authority, studies his
quarry and smiles. The phone rings.

                    STROGANOV (O.C.)
          Demidovsky, I can't find the
          police station's number.

                    DEMIDOVSKY
          Yes, I have it.

He leaves the office with a notebook. Vovo wastes no time
to loosen the knots tying them together. Grigor and Vovo
jump up and race for the exit. Grigor knows the quickest
way out of the Palace grounds.

EXT. THE PALACE GARDENS LEADING TO THE SOUTHERN GATE -
NIGHT

They race for the gate leading to the public road.

                                        DISSOLVE TO:

INT. NOVY PETERHOF RAIL STATION - NIGHT

Grigor and Vovo arrive out of breath at the station, and
see a train waiting. They climb aboard and the train
pulls off.

                                        CUT TO:

INT. THE TRAIN CARRIAGE - NIGHT

                    GRIGOR
          I'm in deep trouble. They'll be
          on my trail in no time.

                    VOVO
          What will happen to me? If you
          don't involve me they won't find
          me, I'll make sure of that.

                    GRIGOR
          You have a better chance of not
          getting caught, you have no
          fixed address.

                    VOVO
          Well, thank my lucky stars for
          that. You won't tell them where
          we met, will you?

                    GRIGOR
          No need to worry.

                    VOVO
          And what about the paintings you
          left in a locker? That person
          will be your accessory, and in
          for trouble as well.

                    GRIGOR
          I'll take care of that. That
          person is Lara who will stand by
          me, regardless. Hey, I've lost
          the watch she gave me.

                    VOVO
          No you haven't. I'll swop it for
          what you owe me, plus a bit
          extra for going beyond the call
          of duty.

                    GRIGOR
              (ruffles Vovo's hair)
          You rascal. I've good mind to
          hand you over to end your
          thieving ways.

                    VOVO
          I'm too far gone for that. In
          any case, its the only way I can
          look after myself.

                    GRIGOR
          Here's what I owe you, and a bit
                    (MORE)

                    GRIGOR (CONT'D)
          extra. Maybe I'll still have to
          call on your criminal skills to
          complete the job.

                    VOVO
          Don't count on it! We can get
          off here. It's Baltiysky stop.

                                        CUT TO:

INT. BALTIYSKY STATION - NIGHT

Grigor and Vovo get off the train. With both hands Vovo
shakes Grigor's hand and disappears up the stairs and out
of Grigor's life.

                                        FADE OUT:

                                        FADE TO:

INT. LARA'S APARTMENT ST PETERSBURG - NIGHT

Grigor knocks on Lara's door, and she let's him in. They
don't speak, but get into bed. Grigor huddles up close to
her and cannot sleep as his mind races over the events of
the night.

                                        CUT TO:

INT. LARA'S APARTMENT ST PETERSBURG - DAY

Lara makes coffee while Grigor sits at the table waiting
for her.

                    LARA
          You're so quiet Grigor. Is there
          anything you should be telling
          me?

                    GRIGOR
          I'm in trouble. I have to get to
          Moscow and away from St
          Petersburg.

                    LARA
          You're not going to confide in
          me?

Grigor begins to sob uncontrollably. Lara goes to console
him.

                    LARA (CONT'D)
Grigor?

                    GRIGOR
I am sorry, Lara, really sorry.

                    LARA
Why? What have you done for you
to apologise to me?

                    GRIGOR
I've implicated you and you too
could be in trouble.

                    LARA
Now you have to tell me the
truth!

                    GRIGOR
I was caught in the Palace last
night in the Rotari room. As you
know I was going to replace the
paintings of Tatyana with my
replicas. But Stroganov caught
me.

                    LARA
How can that implicate me?

                    GRIGOR
My paintings are in the red
canister in your locker.

INT. MISHA'S PLACE OF WORK MOSCOW - DAY

Misha is at his drawing board. The office secretary
brings him his messages.

                    SECRETARY
These urgent messages arrived
while you were on holiday at the
Black Sea, Mikhail. Looks like
the SRP criminal services of the
MVD is more than interested in
you.

INT. THE SRP HEADQUARTERS MOSCOW - DAY

Misha is ushered into a sparsely furnished interrogation
room with grey walls. A *syshchik*, Detective Skuratov, a
large and burly much bemedalled officer is waiting for
him. He has a heavy Stalinesque moustache and black hair,
but the resemblance stops there.

                    SKURATOV
                (gestures to Misha)
        Sit.

Skuratov lights up a cheroot.

                    SKURATOV (CONT'D)
                You are Mikhail Ivanovich. Do
                you know who I am?

                    MISHA
                No Sir.

                    SKURATOV
                I am head of the SRP and in
                charge of crimes involving
                Russian art treasures.

                    MISHA
                I hope I can be of service, Sir,
                although I have no idea why I am
                here.

                    SKURATOV
                (wheezing through the smoke)
                You will soon, Ivanovich...soon
                enough.'

A policeman takes notes. Skuratov leans across and tells
him to start.

                    SKURATOV (CONT'D)
                Now answer the questions first.
                Later it will be your turn. The
                artist, Grigor Anatoly Sidorov,
                is well known to you? Is that
                correct?

                    MISHA
                (cautiously)
                Yes, that is so.

                    SKURATOV
                That man is in deep trouble. Did
                you know that?

                    MISHA
                (shakes his head)
                No Sir, that is news to me.

                    SKURATOV
                That might not be a bad thing,
                because then he might come out
                of hiding and contact you,
                knowing that you are unaware of
                his crime.

                    MISHA
          May I ask...?

                    SKURATOV
               (puts his finger to his
               lips)
          Shush...you can talk later. He
          is an artist, and highly praised
          for his work. The Art Academy
          holds him in high esteem, and
          the Department of Art Treasures
          where he used to work endorses
          his competence. But, he has gone
          beyond what can be expected of
          one so highly regarded. One
          month ago he managed to enter
          one of Russia's treasuries after
          hours and without authority. He
          and a much younger accomplice
          were held briefly, but through
          the incompetence of the security
          guard they escaped. I must say
          that in my day, that guard would
          be paying for that mistake with
          his life.

Skuratov stubs out the offensive cheroot.

                    SKURATOV (CONT'D)
          Does what I tell you seem like
          the man you know?

                    MISHA
          It most certainly does not,
          Sir...,

                    SKURATOV
          When did you last see him?

                    MISHA
          It was more than a month ago. We
          met for coffee.

                    SKURATOV
          Where?

                    MISHA
          A coffee bar near the Kremlin.

                    SKURATOV
          Did anyone see you together?

                    MISHA
          Not that I'm aware of.

Skuratov studies his quarry cynically and tilts back his chair against the wall.

                    SKURATOV
          Do you know of any place he
          could be hiding?

                    MISHA
          No, absolutely no. Have you,
          Sir, interviewed the Staff at
          the Peterhof Palace. They were
          in daily contact with him during
          his assignment there.

                    SKURATOV
               (accusing)
          What assignment? Why don't we
          know about this.

                    MISHA
          The Department of Art Treasures
          assigned Mr Sidorov to undertake
          a rigorous study of the
          paintings of the Palace over a
          year ago. He was often there for
          weeks at a time, carrying out
          his work.

                    SKURATOV
               (angry)
          Well I'll be damned. That means
          that he must have had
          authorisation to be in the
          Palace at some stage, which
          completely changes our line of
          investigation. Heads will roll
          over this. What more do you
          know?

                    MISHA
          I can't add anything more of
          relevance.

There is a pause as Skuratov makes a note.

                    SKURATOV
          That will be all, Ivanovich. But
          we will keep tabs on you, as you
          are the closest friend our
          Sidorov seems to have. Sooner or
          later, he will be in touch with
          you. Of that I am sure. Be gone
          with you, and I expect you to
          come running should you find out
          anything which could help us
               (MORE)

                    SKURATOV (CONT'D)
          find a criminal, whether he is
          your friend or not. You do
          realise that harbouring a
          criminal, not only physically,
          makes a person an accessory?

                                              FADE OUT:

                                              FADE TO:

INT. MISHA'S APARTMENT IN A SOVIET BLOCK - DAY

Misha is eating at a table.

                    MISHA (V.O.)
          After the interview with
          Skuratov of the SRP, I am
          wondering how Grigor is coping
          without Lara's help, and for
          that matter without mine. We are
          the two people closest to him,
          and I have not had word from him
          ever since our last meeting some
          time before. With all his next-
          of-kin out of the country, a
          familial sanctuary does not
          exist. There is only one
          solution...take the train out to
          Kolomenskoye, and descend on his
          dacha without warning. The fact
          that he hasn't called me could
          mean that he is hoping his trail
          would run cold, and that any
          contact with me might offer a
          lead to the authorities as to
          his whereabouts. Since Skuratov
          has warned that his unit would
          keep tabs on me, I have to be
          extra careful not to open the
          way to them finding Grigor.
          Also, for me to contact Lara
          would not be intelligent, as it
          would link her with me. It is,
          as it were, a game of cat and
          mouse, a situation I have never
          been in before. I am aware that
          everything I do in my effort to
          locate Grigor, could conceivably
          offer clues to those he is
          trying to evade. Skuratov has
          warned that if I harbour any
          information about Grigor's
          whereabouts, then I will become
                    (MORE)

                    MISHA (CONT'D)
          an accessory. For the sake of my
          conscience, I have to make a
          pact with myself...if my loyalty
          to Grigor has to come at a
          price, then so be it.

INT. MISHA'S APARTMENT IN A SOVIET BLOCK - NIGHT

The telephone rings.

                    MISHA
          Hullo.

                    VOICE
          Is that Mikhail Ivanovich?

                    MISHA
          It is. Who is that?

                    OLGA
          This is Olga. I have a message
          from a friend of a friend.
          Please, I want to meet you at
          the Olympic coffee bar. It is a
          crowded place, but that would be
          a good thing.

                    MISHA
          When?

                    OLGA
          Tomorrow at ten in the morning?

                    MISHA
          I'll be there. But how will I
          recognise you?

                    VOICE
          I will wear a cream scarf with a
          blue stripe.

                                        CUT TO:

INT. OLYMPIC COFFEE BAR MOSCOW

Misha sits waiting and sees a girl entering. She has a
cream head scarf with the blue stripe. He raises his hand
and Lara nods and goes to the self-service bar before
joining him.

                    LARA
Misha. By now you will know I am
Lara.

                    MISHA
I can see why Grigor is so
smitten with you. It is my
pleasure to meet you at last.

                    LARA
I love Moscow. It is such a
vibrant place and is part of the
New Russia. St Petersburg, with
its layers of history, still
resides nostalgically in its
past.

                    MISHA
Understandable.

                    LARA
Yes. But I am here about Grigor,
as you have no doubt realised. I
have not had word from Grigor
since we parted on a fateful
morning in St Petersburg, and I
am worried about him. You know
about his crime of unlawfully
entering the Palace, and what
was worse, with a street boy
with a history of thieving.

                    MISHA
Yes, and I have been questioned
by the SRP Head as to his
whereabouts.

                    LARA
Probably because you are his
close friend, Misha, and not
about Grigor's paintings of
Tatyana of the Rotari
collection. Have you seen them?

                    MISHA
In ignorance of any crime, I
have seen them, at the dacha. I
think they are superb copies,
but why are they central to this
whole saga?

                    LARA
        (confidentially)
Those four paintings were
painted with a purpose. Grigor's
            (MORE)

LARA (CONT'D)

plan is to replace the original
paintings of the same Tatyana
Menshikov in the Rotari Room
with his own paintings. He would
then own four original paintings
of one of his presumed ancestors
done by a famed artist, Pietro
Rotari. His work is so good that
I doubt if anyone ever would
know the difference.

MISHA

I cannot believe that my
lifelong and close friend is
capable of such treachery. I
find that beyond belief, Lara.
You will agree I'm sure that
Russian treasures belong to the
people, not to one single
individual.

LARA

Not long ago, I thought that way
too, but I have changed my mind.
Look down the road of history,
how ethical have politicians
been, and the *boyars*, for that
matter, about expropriating
Russian treasures for
themselves, their own private
enjoyment? History is studded
with acts of crimes against the
Russian people. Grigor's family
were stripped, dispossessed, and
died for what they believed
in...his grandfather, Anatoly
for instance. They were harmless
people, good Russians.

MISHA

So you're saying that by
entering the Peterhof Palace at
night without authorisation, and
with an accomplice, Grigor was
in the process of carrying out a
bigger plan...retribution for
the States crimes against his
family?

LARA

Yes, crimes against his family
involving dispossession, and,
because they were from the noble
class at the time of political
change, by a Bolshevik
                    (MORE)

                    LARA (CONT'D)
government. Almost by default
they were cast as White
Russians, and faced persecution,
even execution.

                    MISHA
Whew, you make a good case for
Grigor's misconduct.

                    LARA
I do, Misha. And what's more I
have decided I want to help him
achieve his goal.

                    MISHA
Your are willing to step into
the unethical world which Grigor
has chosen?

                    LARA
You and I are Grigor's closest
friends. I love him
unconditionally, but I put it to
you, is your love unconditional
as well?

                    MISHA
I believe so...I will always
remain loyal to him no matter
what.

                    LARA
Well, let me put you to a test,
Mikhail. Can I trust you
implicitly with a secret which
not even Grigor knows about at
this stage?

                    MISHA
Why confide in me before you
confide in him, Lara. That would
be connivance surely?

                    LARA
No, what I have in mind is for
his benefit, and for that matter
for mine, in another way.

                    MISHA
Now you're speaking in riddles.

                    LARA
Well, then. Since I want to
marry Grigor one day, I want to
                    (MORE)

LARA (CONT'D)
be part of him, everything he
does, even everything he might
do wrong. I want to be there for
him, Mikhail.

MISHA
Now you're sounding dramatic.

LARA
Life is a drama, I don't have to
tell you. It is how you play out
the drama within your own world
that counts. You have to grow to
live, and if your growth is
inhibited by the baggage from
the past, then you must be
released from your burden.
Anyway, that's how I look at
things. So, I am completing the
task of replacing the four
Pietro Rotari paintings with
Grigor's...the ones he left in
my locker...

MISHA
What?

LARA
Yes, I knew that would shock
you. Now tell me, are you able
to keep that secret? It comes
back to a question of
unconditional love for Grigor,
and your loyalty. Would you wish
for him that the baggage of his
family's past is removed from
his overwilling shoulders?

MISHA
Of course. What do you want me
to do?

LARA
Do nothing, except try to
communicate with Grigor, and
find out how he is. Also, you
must swear secrecy if I am to
carry out this task to its
conclusion. In the meantime, I
don't want Grigor to know about
what I am planning to do. He
would feel very guilty having
someone else becoming more than
(MORE)

                    LARA (CONT'D)
          an accessory, an accomplice in
          fact, which is what it would
          amount to.

Lara takes Misha's hand and squeezes it in solidarity.

                    MISHA
          You can count on me.

                    MISHA (V.O.)
          I was hooked. I am beginning to
          understand Lara's logic and the
          depth of her love for Grigor.
          She is indeed formidable, in a
          feminine sense, in fighting for
          what she wants... Grigor.

                                        FADE OUT:

                                        FADE TO:

EXT. THE RAILWAY STATION TO KOLOMENSKOYE - DAY

Misha borrows a bike from the stationmaster to ride to
the dacha to make contact with Grigor.

                                        CUT TO:

EXT. MARIYA SIDOROVA'S DACHA KOLOMENSKOYE - DAY

Misha knocks on the door of the dacha. He tries three
times each time knocking harder, but gets no response.

                                        CUT TO:

INT. MARIYA SIDOROVA'S DACHA KOLOMENSKOYE - DAY

Grigor goes to the window to see who is knocking, then
seeing Misha slumps to the floor and sobs.

                                        DISSOLVE:

INT. MISHA'S APARTMENT IN A SOVIET BLOCK - DAY

The phone rings. It is Skuratov.

                    SKURATOV
               (formal)
          Ivanovich? We'd like to see you
          again. You've been very quiet
          and I thought it would be a good
          idea just to have another chat
          about your wanderings. Come in
          this afternoon at three o'clock.
          I want you to meet one of my
          staff.

                                        CUT TO:

INT. SRP HEADQUARTERS MOSCOW - DAY

With Skuratov is another officer from MUR, the Moscow
Criminal Intelligence Unit.

                    SKURATOV
          As you see, the net is now
          wider. MUR is just as interested
          as we are to find your friend,
          Mr Sidorov.

They shake hands.

                    SKURATOV (CONT'D)
          When we last met, you undertook
          to offer us any clue as to the
          whereabouts of the fugitive,
          Grigor Sidorov. Not so?

                    MISHA
               (nods)
          Yes.

                    SKURATOV
          Well, if you didn't know it
          then, I am going to tell you
          now...you have two shadows! One
          is your own, and the other
          belongs to the SRP!

Skuratov and the MUR officer enjoy the joke.

                    MISHA
          I am not sure exactly what you
          mean, Sir.

                    SKURATOV
          What were you doing in
          Kolomenskoye, last Saturday to
          be exact?

                    MISHA
                  (hastily)
          Just visiting.

                    SKURATOV
          Well, then. Whose dacha was that
          which you visited on Saturday?

                    MISHA
          I suddenly remembered, Sir, that
          Mr Sidorov's grandmother once
          owned a dacha in Kolomenskoye,
          and since I had not had word
          from him for months now...and I
          had nothing else to do on the
          weekend...I took my chances and
          went to see if I could find him.

                    SKURATOV
          Go on, Ivanovich.

                    MISHA
          I didn't want to waste the
          police's precious time, so I
          undertook that journey more to
          satisfy my curiosity as his
          friend. Of course I would have
          urged him to turn himself in.
          There was no one there and I
          don't even know if Mr Sidorov
          owns the dacha any more.

                    SKURATOV
          Hmm. Very glib. In the meantime
          we have established that the
          dacha is indeed owned by
          Sidorov, an inheritance from his
          babushka, Mariya Sidorova. So
          now we have the house under
          permanent surveillance. Perhaps
          I should be thanking you for
          your unwitting assistance!

Misha is shown to the door.

                                              CUT TO:

EXT. STREET IN MOSCOW - DAY

Misha walks deep in thought.

                    MISHA (O.C.)
          The interview is over at the
          police precinct and I have a lot
                  (MORE)

MISHA (O.C.)(CONT'D)
to think about. Grigor's
disappearance causes me great
anxiety. His mood swings over
the past year have been
symptomatic of something more
troubling, in fact delusionary.
Maybe with the police providing
round the clock surveillance,
they will find him before his
condition deteriorates. At the
rate he is going, he won't be
able to defend his actions in
court nor expect clemency. In
fact he could end up in a mental
institution, which would be the
end of his career as a talented
artist and tantamount to a
living death. Not a prospect I
would wish on my friend.

                                    FADE OUT:

                                    FADE TO:

EXT. BELOW THE MENSHIKOV TOWER CHURCH OF ST GABRIEL
MOSCOW - DAY

Grigor sits awkwardly on the ledge and stares down at the
growing crowd below. People have begun to assemble and
shout and wave. A wailing of sirens in the distance comes
ever closer. He yawns, weary from lack of sleep.

          FIRE CHIEF
Grigor Sidorov, you will go back
inside and come down. The tower
is out of bounds. I will give
you ten minutes to do as I say,
otherwise you will be taken into
custody by force and charged
with illegal occupation of a
sacred place. Do you hear me?

INT. MISHA'S PLACE OF WORK MOSCOW - DAY

Misha is working at his drawing board. The phone rings.

          MISHA
     Hullo.

          SKURATOV
     Have you listened to the morning
               (MORE)

                    SKURATOV (CONT'D)
          news on radio, Ivanovich? We
          believe it is your friend who is
          poised to jump from the
          Menshikov tower. Sidorov is
          sitting high up on a ledge at
          the belfry of the tower. He is
          not responding to any attempt to
          talk him down. We need you there
          my friend. I'll send someone to
          fetch you right away.

INT. POLICE CAR WITH MOTORCYCLE ESCORT MOSCOW- DAY

They drive at breakneck speed in and out of rush hour
traffic, sirens blaring to clear the way. Nearing the
Menshikov tower, Misha can see a figure, Grigor, perched
precariously on the ledge, high up under the belfry arch.
His legs dangle over the edge. Fire ladders are extended
full length to within metres of Grigor.

EXT. BELOW THE MENSHIKOV TOWER CHURCH OF ST GABRIEL
MOSCOW - DAY

Misha leaves the police car and is introduced to the Fire
Chief who has a loud hailer.

                    FIRE CHIEF
          He's in another world. I have
          given him ample warning to come
          down. If we can't get through to
          him, its been suggested we force
          him to go inside the tower using
          the fire hoses...

                    MISHA
          No! Not that! I'll go up the
          ladder and speak to him.

Misha is given a two-way radio and starts up the ladder.
He gets close to Grigor who is dressed in a nightshirt
and is barefoot. His face has no expression, his hair
matted and long and his eyes are unseeing, even when
Misha reaches him.

                    MISHA (CONT'D)
          Grigor, my good friend. I've
          been missing you. Why are you
          sitting here?

                    GRIGOR
          Saint Gabriel told me to.

Grigor looks away not showing any recognition. He fidgets in his pockets and pulls out the Menshikov amber seal. He holds it up to the light and admires it.

                    MISHA
          Grigor,are you listening to your
          old friend?

                    GRIGOR
          Yes.

                    MISHA
          What about we go inside the
          tower, and talk. I'll order
          coffee and your favourite
          pirozhki, remember, with the
          mutton filling?

Misha looks down at the gathering crowd.

                    MISHA (O.C.) (CONT'D)
          The adrenalin pumps through my
          veins. Grigor's delusionary
          state has worsened since the
          incident at the Peterhof Palace.
          It is a miracle that he's found
          his way back to the dacha, let
          alone to the Menshikov tower. I
          know I am dealing not with the
          person I have known since
          boyhood, but someone who has
          undergone a severe mental
          transformation, thanks to an
          obsession which has invaded his
          very being. It's brought on a
          psychotic state and has led him
          to this.

                    GRIGOR
               (shows sudden
                recognition)
          Misha? What are you doing here?

                    MISHA
               (tearful)
          I've come to visit you.

                    GRIGOR
          Come inside. That ladder looks
          very unsteady.

                    MISHA
          Thanks. It'll be nice to chat
          again. Here, give me a hand.

Grigor reaches forward but is unable to reach Misha's outstretched hand. The crowd below, seeing movement, let out an audible gasp.

                                              CUT TO:

INT. INSIDE THE BELFRY OF THE MENSHIKOV TOWER MOSCOW - DAY

Grigor and Misha move to sit in a place in the corner away from the sight of the panicking world below.

                    MISHA
          What brings you here, Grigor?

                    GRIGOR
          I wondered when you'd ask.
          Well...it was the faded sepia
          print of a tall tower in a
          photograph on the wall of the
          dacha which led me here. It was
          as though I was seeing it for
          the first time. I suddenly
          remembered my dedushka, Anatoly
          Sidorov, telling me about that
          tower, the Menshikov tower
          outside Moscow, over the church
          of St Gabriel. Then, do you
          remember that photograph in a
          giltframe of St Gabriel,
          depicted as an angel with wings
          spread, flying through clouds of
          white?

                    MISHA
          Mmm, yes, I always thought it
          too sentimental.

                    GRIGOR
          Somehow those two pictures had
          new meaning. I was scared of
          what would happen to me and I
          saw a way out. I would fly away,
          like St Gabriel, and the
          Menshikov tower was compelling
          as it had the right association
          with my family.

Grigor starts to sob, his body shaking as his conscious mind re-asserts itself and he realises how close he has been to death. Misha puts his arms around his friend until his convulsions subside and he wipes the tears from his eyes. The two-way radio breaks into a crackling sound.

                    FIRE CHIEF
          Ivanovich. What is going on
          there? Over.

                    MISHA
          Things are improving. I believe
          that we shall be spending the
          night up here or as long as Mr
          Sidorov needs. We shall be
          needing blankets and food. Over.

                    FIRE CHIEF
               (in frustration)
          This is most irregular. What are
          your needs? Over.

                    MISHA
               (smiles)
          Clothes, blankets, food for
          two...and make that mutton
          pirozhki, and flasks of tea.
          Over.

                                        CUT TO:

EXT. BELOW THE MENSHIKOV TOWER CHURCH OF ST GABRIEL
MOSCOW - NIGHT

At the bottom of the Menshikov tower the assembly swells
with onlookers, hoping to satisfy their ghoulish
curiosity with an actual suicide. Apart from the police,
more media vans have taken up positions. Floodlights
which illuminate the tower, and the logos of the national
television broadcaster and other channels are evident.

                    MISHA
          I went to find you at the dacha,
          Grigor. Where have you been?

                    GRIGOR
          I've been on the run, Misha.
          When you came to the cottage,
          and knocked, I was there, but I
          didn't want to see anyone. Why
          was I hiding away from my friend
          Misha? Should I have opened the
          door? If I confided in you,
          Misha, you would become an
          accessory to my crime? Then,
          perhaps you had news of Lara, or
          perhaps you both had been
          accused of harbouring a
          criminal. The stress of letting
          my friends down was unbearable.

                              MISHA
            You haven't let us down, Grigor.

                              GRIGOR
            Then I slept for two days
            without going out even to
            restock the larder. That was two
            weeks ago and then the picture
            of the Menshikov tower on the
            wall of the dacha led me to this
            place.

        Their conversation is interrupted by a voice on the two-
        way radio.

                          CHIEF OF POLICE
            Now you listen to Ivanovich, I
            want you to report to me every
            hour. We want Sidorov to come
            down and are all wanting to go
            home. Over.

                              MISHA
            I need more time, but can report
            that there is progress...

        He hears a familiar voice talking to the Chief of Police.

                          CHIEF OF POLICE
            There is a lady here from the
            Department of Art Treasures who
            says she is a friend of Sidorov.
            She wants to speak to him.

                              LARA
            Grigor, are you all right? I'm
            here and want desperately to see
            you. I want to come up. Will
            that be OK?

                              GRIGOR
            Lara!

                              MISHA
            Yes, Lara, come up with the
            tower stairs.

                                              CUT TO:

        INT. INSIDE THE BELFRY OF THE MENSHIKOV TOWER MOSCOW –
        DAY

        Lara arrives at the top, and rushes to Grigor.

                        LARA
          Grigor, I was in St Petersburg
          and saw you on television
          sitting on the ledge. They said
          you were going to be charged.
          Oh, thank God you're all right.

                        MISHA
          You've come at the right time,
          Lara. Grigor needs you. They are
          going to charge him with
          entering the Peterhof palace in
          St Petersburg without
          authorisation. Also with the
          intention to remove certain
          items of Soviet property, and,
          to have permitted access to
          another unauthorised person into
          a national treasury to carry out
          this deed.

                        LARA
          I have a confession to make and
          I did what I did to relieve
          Grigor of the onerous task which
          he had imposed on himself.

Grigor and Misha look questioningly at Lara.

                        GRIGOR
          What have you done, Lara, my
          pet?

                        LARA
          I have replaced the four
          original Rotari paintings of
          Tatyana with your replicas
          Grigor, the ones you left in my
          locker at the Peterhof palace.

                        MISHA
          Lara! What have you done? Do you
          realise that you've compounded
          and worsened the situation for
          Grigor?

                        LARA
          No, you're wrong, Mikhail. In
          fact Grigor cannot be charged
          with replacing the originals
          with the replicas. I'm prepared
          to take the consequences of my
          actions.

                    MISHA
          That could mean imprisonment for
          life.

                    LARA
          I will do anything to relieve
          Grigor of his burden. His work
          as an artist is his lifeblood,
          and he is probably the best fine
          artist today in Russia. His work
          will hang proudly amongst the
          other Rotari paintings and in
          other galleries one day. I love
          him and want to see him well
          again. And you, Mikhail? Think
          of yourself, not of me. Now that
          your are party to what I have
          done, will you turn me in?

Misha shakes his head in solidarity.

                    MISHA
          I believe that you are the only
          one who can help him to rejoin
          the real world.

Grigor reaches for them both and brings them together in
a hug.

                    GRIGOR
          Please don't make me feel
          obliged to either of you, my
          only two friends. What Lara has
          done for me is the measure of
          her love. I shall love her even
          more for that. I know I'm sick,
          and have caused enough trouble
          to both of you over my stupid
          bungling. I have to give myself
          up and am prepared to pay back
          my debt to the Russian people.

The two lovers embrace. Misha looks away to allow them
their moment of reconciliation.

                    LARA
          Grigor promises me he will give
          himself up and undergo
          treatment. We can't ask for
          more.

Grigor removes the amber seal from his pocket, and shows
it to Misha and Lara.

                    GRIGOR
          One last thing...I believe I
          have finally put the family's
          Menshikov connection into its
          historical context and I have
          Tatyana to thank for that. I
          feel more lucid now and, with
          your support, ready for the law
          to take its course.

Grigor returns the amber seal to his pocket and they
descend the stair of the tower together.

                                        CUT TO:

EXT. BELOW THE MENSHIKOV TOWER CHURCH OF ST GABRIEL
MOSCOW - DAY

Grigor, Misha and Lara emerge from the base of the tower
to be confronted by a media frenzy.

                    REPORTER
          We want your story, Grigor. Why
          did you do it? What is going
          through your mind now?

                    REPORTER 1
          Was it for love, Grigor? We want
          your story.

Grigor is handcuffed and hustled into a police car
followed by a convoy of media vehicles.

                                        FADE TO:

EXT. MOSCOW POLICE HEADQUARTERS PETROVKA - DAY

The convoy arrives at the headquarters and the heavy
doors giving access to the courtyard of the headquarters
are opened. Reporters and camera men stream in before the
police can stop them. Grigor is taken to the charge
office.

INT. MOSCOW POLICE HEADQUARTERS PETROVKA - DAY

Misha and Lara are swept along with the crowd into a
lobby of the police station where Grigor is maneouvred
into the holding cage, a byzantine prison tradition where
prisoners down the ages are held and made to endure the
taunts of the masses.

                    MISHA (O.C.)

I have been concerned about
Grigor's mental stability but he
seems to have a healthy
detachment from the frenzied mob
outside his temporary
incarceration.

                    CHARGE OFFICER
Grigor Anatoly Sidorov, you are
charged with entering the
Peterhof palace in St Petersburg
without authorisation. You are
also charged with the intention
to remove certain items of
property belonging to the
Russian people, and to have
permitted access to another
person into a national treasury
to carry out this deed. You will
face these charges in a St
Petersburg court, but in the
meantime you will be held in a
temporary containment cell until
your transfer can be arranged.

                                                    CUT TO:

INT. THE COURT HOUSE IN ST PETERSBURG - DAY

Grigor stands in the dock.

                    MISHA (V.O.)
The defence in Grigor's trial is
dealing mainly with his state of
mind at the time of his criminal
action. Also, the prosecution is
not able not uncover any motive
for his unauthorised entry into
the Peterhof Palace on that
fateful night. Who the person
was who had accompanied him, the
young boy, and his role, remains
a blank on the record book. His
chance encounter with Vovo has
left Grigor none the wiser as to
where the boy lives, or what his
real name is. Due to the doubts
about Grigor's state of mind, he
has been subjected to
psychological examination prior
                    (MORE)

to the trial and diagnosed as
being prone to psychotic
episodes and bipolar disorder.
Based on the outcome, the
defence has argued that he
suffers from a fixed false
belief and fanciful self-
delusion. The fact that he is an
artist of recognised talent has
tended to mitigate in his favour
with the court. But the
defence's claim as to his
delusionary spells provides the
best defence against his
permanent incarceration. About
the Menshikov connection, the
court seems disinterested in
such a private affair, not
having the evidence to link his
crime with the removal and
replacement of the Tatyana
paintings. Lara has been shrewd
in covering their tracks and
bringing that aspect of Grigor's
deception to closure. The
newshounds will have a field
day, reporting every last word
and newspaper sales will rocket.
Due to the extensive news
coverage, readers have been in
the court room by proxy every
day of the trial. An unexpected
development is the groundswell
of sympathy which has emerged.
The public has turned around the
legalese and legal grandstanding
and found that humanity has been
on trial, not a criminal act.
This attitude has finally
determined Grigor's sentence...a
single year in prison. Had the
public known about Lara's
selfless act of love and the
replacing of the eighteenth
century Pietro Rotari paintings
of Tatyana with those of fine
artist Grigor Sidorov, the
outcome would undoubtedly have
been different. What the public
does not know will remain our
secret.

                                    FADE TO:

INT. ST GABRIEL CHAPEL ONE YEAR LATER - DAY

Grigor and Lara marry at a private ceremony in the St
Gabriel chapel under the Menshikov tower.

                                              DISSOLVE:

INT. MARIYA SIDOROVA'S DACHA KOLOMENSKOYE - DAY

Grigor and Lara have returned from honeymoon. Misha is
visiting them at the dacha and is busy studying the four
paintings of Tatyana on the walls of the living space.

                    MISHA (V.O.)
          Grigor has emerged into the real
          world after his year-long
          incarceration in the St
          Petersburg prison. He and Lara
          are now married. This is my
          first visit to the Sidorovs
          after their wedding. For the
          first time I am able to study
          the four paintings of Tatyana
          properly and with renewed
          interest. To the untrained eye,
          the paintings are impossible to
          tell apart from Rotari's
          paintings and it is difficult to
          choose between them for the
          sheer natural beauty which each
          one portrays. Has Lara or has
          she not really done what she
          claimed...that she's swapped
          Grigor's paintings with those of
          Rotari? Is Lara capable of such
          deception, I ask myself? It is
          impossible to tell, as her love
          for Grigor is so great that she
          might have decided that his
          return to health depends on him
          believing that his plan is
          complete.

Grigor and Lara stand quietly in the background
watching as Misha moves back and forth between
paintings. He stops at one and then looks at Lara.

                    MISHA (V.O)(CONT'D)
          Only Lara would ever know if
          these paintings here on the
          walls of the dacha are indeed
          the Rotari originals. This one
          of Tatyana I consider to be the
          best and I've been studying it
                    (MORE)

                    MISHA (V.O.)(CONT'D)
          for some minutes. Then, just
          now, as I was about to turn
          away, I thought I saw Tatyana
          wink at me. It's only happened
          once, and is a lesson to me that
          delusion has the power beyond
          our comprehension to bring the
          impossible into reality.

                                              THE END

www.ingramcontent.com/pod-product-compliance
Lightning Source LLC
Chambersburg PA
CBHW081549170526
45166CB00009B/2630